CliffsN

Cisneros

The House on Mango Street & "Woman Hollering Creek" and Other Stories

y Mary Patterson Thornburg, Ph.D.

IN THIS BOOK

- Learn about the Life and Background of the Author
- Preview an Introduction to the Works
- Study a graphical Character Map for *The House on Mango Street*
- Explore themes and literary devices in the Critical Commentaries
- Examine in-depth Character Analyses
- Enhance your understanding of the works with Critical Essays
- Reinforce what you learn with CliffsNotes Review
- Find additional information to further your study in CliffsNotes Resource Center and online at www.cliffsnotes.com

IDG BOOKS WORLDWIDE

IDG Books Worldwide, Inc.
An International Data Group Company
Foster City, CA • Chicago, IL • Indianapolis, IN • New York, NY

About the Author

Mary Patterson Thornburg attended Holy Names College, Spokane, WA, and took her undergraduate degree from Montana State University. She holds the M.A. and Ph.D. from Ball State University, where she taught English until 1998; she lives with her husband, Thomas Thornburg, in Montana.

Author's Acknowledgment: Bridget Kevane, Assistant Professor of Modern Languages and Literatures at Montana State University Bozeman, was most helpful in providing translations for the Glossaries in this guide. *Gracias.*

Publisher's Acknowledgments
Editorial

Project Editor: Tracy Barr

Acquisitions Editor: Greg Tubach

Glossary Editors: The editors and staff at Webster's New World™ Dictionaries

Editorial Administrator: Michelle Hacker

Production

Indexer: York Production Services, Inc.

Proofreader: York Production Services, Inc.

IDG Books Indianapolis Production Department

CliffsNotes™ Cisneros' *The House on Mango Street* & *"Woman Hollering Creek" and Other Stories*

Published by
IDG Books Worldwide, Inc.
An International Data Group Company
919 E. Hillsdale Blvd.
Suite 300
Foster City, CA 94404
www.idgbooks.com (IDG Books Worldwide Web site)
www.cliffsnotes.com (CliffsNotes Web site)

Note: If you purchased this book without a cover, you should be aware that this book is stolen property. It was reported as "unsold and destroyed" to the publisher, and neither the author nor the publisher has received any payment for this "stripped book."

Copyright © 2001 IDG Books Worldwide, Inc. All rights reserved. No part of this book, including interior design, cover design, and icons, may be reproduced or transmitted in any form, by any means (electronic, photocopying, recording, or otherwise) without the prior written permission of the publisher.

Library of Congress Control Number: 00-107797

ISBN: 0-7645-8653-X

Printed in the United States of America

10 9 8 7 6 5 4 3 2 1

1O/QX/RS/QQ/IN

Distributed in the United States by IDG Books Worldwide, Inc.

Distributed by CDG Books Canada Inc. for Canada; by Transworld Publishers Limited in the United Kingdom; by IDG Norge Books for Norway; by IDG Sweden Books for Sweden; by IDG Books Australia Publishing Corporation Pty. Ltd. for Australia and New Zealand; by TransQuest Publishers Pte Ltd. for Singapore, Malaysia, Thailand, Indonesia, and Hong Kong; by Gotop Information Inc. for Taiwan; by ICG Muse, Inc. for Japan; by Norma Comunicaciones S.A. for Columbia; by Intersoft for South Africa; by Eyrolles for France; by International Thomson Publishing for Germany, Austria and Switzerland; by Distribuidora Cuspide for Argentina; by LR International for Brazil; by Galileo Libros for Chile; by Ediciones ZETA S.C.R. Ltda. for Peru; by WS Computer Publishing Corporation, Inc., for the Philippines; by Contemporanea de Ediciones for Venezuela; by Express Computer Distributors for the Caribbean and West Indies; by Micronesia Media Distributor, Inc. for Micronesia; by Grupo Editorial Norma S.A. for Guatemala; by Chips Computadoras S.A. de C.V. for Mexico; by Editorial Norma de Panama S.A. for Panama; by American Bookshops for Finland. Authorized Sales Agent: Anthony Rudkin Associates for the Middle East and North Africa.

For general information on IDG Books Worldwide's books in the U.S., please call our Consumer Customer Service department at **800-762-2974**. For reseller information, including discounts and premium sales, please call our Reseller Customer Service department at **800-434-3422**.

For information on where to purchase IDG Books Worldwide's books outside the U.S., please contact our International Sales department at **317-572-3993** or fax **317-572-4002**.

For consumer information on foreign language translations, please contact our Customer Service department at **1-800-434-3422**, fax **317-572-4002**, or e-mail rights@idgbooks.com.

For information on licensing foreign or domestic rights, please phone **+1-650-653-7098**.

For sales inquiries and special prices for bulk quantities, please contact our Order Services department at **800-434-3422** or write to the address above.

For information on using IDG Books Worldwide's books in the classroom or for ordering examination copies, please contact our Educational Sales department at **800-434-2086** or fax **317-572-4005**.

For press review copies, author interviews, or other publicity information, please contact our Public Relations department at **650-653-7000** or fax **650-653-7500**.

For authorization to photocopy items for corporate, personal, or educational use, please contact Copyright Clearance Center, 222 Rosewood Drive, Danvers, MA 01923, or fax **978-750-4470**.

LIMIT OF LIABILITY/DISCLAIMER OF WARRANTY: THE PUBLISHER AND AUTHOR HAVE USED THEIR BEST EFFORTS IN PREPARING THIS BOOK. THE PUBLISHER AND AUTHOR MAKE NO REPRESENTATIONS OR WARRANTIES WITH RESPECT TO THE ACCURACY OR COMPLETENESS OF THE CONTENTS OF THIS BOOK AND SPECIFICALLY DISCLAIM ANY IMPLIED WARRANTIES OF MERCHANTABILITY OR FITNESS FOR A PARTICULAR PURPOSE. THERE ARE NO WARRANTIES WHICH EXTEND BEYOND THE DESCRIPTIONS CONTAINED IN THIS PARAGRAPH. NO WARRANTY MAY BE CREATED OR EXTENDED BY SALES REPRESENTATIVES OR WRITTEN SALES MATERIALS. THE ACCURACY AND COMPLETENESS OF THE INFORMATION PROVIDED HEREIN AND THE OPINIONS STATED HEREIN ARE NOT GUARANTEED OR WARRANTED TO PRODUCE ANY PARTICULAR RESULTS, AND THE ADVICE AND STRATEGIES CONTAINED HEREIN MAY NOT BE SUITABLE FOR EVERY INDIVIDUAL. NEITHER THE PUBLISHER NOR AUTHOR SHALL BE LIABLE FOR ANY LOSS OF PROFIT OR ANY OTHER COMMERCIAL DAMAGES, INCLUDING BUT NOT LIMITED TO SPECIAL, INCIDENTAL, CONSEQUENTIAL, OR OTHER DAMAGES.

Trademarks: Cliffs, CliffsNotes, CliffsNotes, Inc. logo and all related logos and trade dress are registered trademarks or trademarks of IDG Books Worldwide, Inc., in the United States and other countries. All other brand names and product names used in this book are trade names, service marks, trademarks, or registered trademarks of their respective owners. IDG Books Worldwide, Inc., is not associated with any product or vendor mentioned in this book.

is a registered trademark under exclusive license to IDG Books Worldwide, Inc. from International Data Group, Inc.

Table of Contents

How to Use This Book

CliffsNotes Cisneros' *The House on Mango Street* & *"Woman Hollering Creek" and Other Stories* supplements the original work, giving you background information about the author, an introduction to the novel, a graphical character map, critical commentaries, expanded glossaries, and a comprehensive index. CliffsNotes Review tests your comprehension of the original text and reinforces learning with questions and answers, practice projects, and more. For further information on Sandra Cisneros and *The House on Mango Street* & *"Woman Hollering Creek" and Other Stories*, check out the CliffsNotes Resource Center.

CliffsNotes provides the following icons to highlight essential elements of particular interest:

Reveals the underlying themes in the work.

Helps you to more easily relate to or discover the depth of a character.

Uncovers elements such as setting, atmosphere, mystery, passion, violence, irony, symbolism, tragedy, foreshadowing, and satire.

Enables you to appreciate the nuances of words and phrases.

Don't Miss Our Web Site

Discover classic literature as well as modern-day treasures by visiting the CliffsNotes Web site at www.cliffsnotes.com. You can obtain a quick download of a CliffsNotes title, purchase a title in print form, browse our catalog, or view online samples.

You'll also find interactive tools that are fun and informative, links to interesting Web sites, tips, articles, and additional resources to help you, not only for literature, but for test prep, finance, careers, computers, and the Internet too. See you at www.cliffsnotes.com!

LIFE AND BACKGROUND OF THE AUTHOR

Early Years and Education

Sandra Cisneros was born December 20, 1954, in Chicago. Although she grew up mainly in Chicago, the family often visited her father's relatives in Mexico, and Cisneros would later say that she felt "displaced" during her childhood. In 1987, Cisneros would tell an interviewer in Texas that she had never felt a strong sense of connection to Chicago. Nevertheless, her book *The House on Mango Street* is set there.

To the same interviewer, Sandra Cisneros expresses a little annoyance at readers who assume that she *is* her *Mango Street* protagonist, Esperanza Cordero—that the book, in other words, is autobiographical. (In a later interview, she calls it "an invented autobiography.") The difference between writing factually about one's own life and writing imaginatively out of one's experience can be subtle, of course, and there are undeniable similarities between the fictional Esperanza and Cisneros, who grew up during the 1950s and 1960s in a working-class Latino family. One obvious difference between them is that Esperanza has three siblings, a sister and two brothers; Cisneros, on the other hand, grew up as the only sister to *six* brothers. One imagines that her mother must have been pleased to have a daughter among so many sons. And, unlike some women in similar situations, Cisneros' mother did not insist that Sandra spend all her time helping with the traditional "women's work," but encouraged her to develop her intellect and imagination by reading. In this respect, certainly, Cisneros' childhood resembles that of her character Esperanza, whose reading as reported in *Mango Street* has included such children's classics as the *Alice* books by Lewis Carroll and Charles Kingsley's *The Water-Babies*. Although her published fiction (to 2000 at least) is firmly realistic, Cisneros conveys a sense of wonder and magic that reveals a grounding not only in folklore but also in these grand old literary fantasies.

Educated in Catholic schools and at Chicago's Loyola University, where she took a B.A. in 1976, Cisneros was admitted to the prestigious Writers' Workshop at the University of Iowa and was awarded the M.F.A. degree in 1978.

Career and Writing

Most of Cisneros' classmates at Iowa were people from more materially privileged backgrounds than Cisneros', descendents of European immigrants to the U.S. Initially, Cisneros attempted to use their kinds of subjects, characters, and settings in her own writing. Unhappy with the results, she then made an important decision: She decided to "rebel" by writing about the neighborhoods in which she had grown up, the people who were her relatives and friends and neighbors. *The House on Mango Street* was begun.

Cisneros did not complete the book for several years, however; meanwhile, she taught high school and served as a college recruiter and minority student counselor. In 1982–83, after winning a National Endowment for the Arts fellowship, Cisneros went to Greece to work on her fiction. After serving as artist-in-residence at Foundation Michael Karolyi in Vence, France, she returned to the U.S. and, in 1984, found a publisher for *Mango Street*: The University of Houston's Arte Público Press. During the following few years, Cisneros held a variety of university positions, always continuing to write both poetry and prose. With the Random House publication in 1991 of *"Woman Hollering Creek" and Other Stories* and the reissuing in the same year of *The House on Mango Street*, the writer became widely known; her books, enthusiastically reviewed, quickly found their way onto reading lists from middle school to university literature classes.

As of September, 2000, Cisneros has published (in book form) no more fiction except for a bilingual expansion for very young readers of a short section from *Mango Street*: *Hairs: Pelitos*, illustrated by Terry Ybanez and published by Knopf. Her books of poetry include *Bad Boys* (Mango Publications, 1980); *My Wicked, Wicked Ways* (Third Woman Press, 1987); and *Loose Woman* (Knopf, 1994). She has contributed to a variety of periodicals, including *Contact II, Glamour, Imagine, Los Angeles Times, New York Times, Revista Chicano-Riquena,* and *Village Voice*.

Recognition and Awards

Cisneros' awards include two National Endowment for the Arts fellowships (1982 and 1988); the American Book Award from the Before Columbus Foundation, for *The House on Mango Street* (1985); the Paisano Dobie Fellowship (1986); first and second prizes in Segundo Concurso Nacional del Cuento Chicano, sponsored by the University of Arizona; the Lannan Foundation Literary Award (1991); an honorary doctorate from the State University of New York at Purchase (1993); and a MacArthur fellowship (1995).

Sandra Cisneros' work has been praised by critics for many reasons, from the authenticity of her characters' voices and experience to the marvelous simplicity of her style. Perhaps more important than critics are ordinary readers, who find Cisneros' writing to be moving, funny, direct, and true on the most basic of human levels. Her fiction, in *The House on Mango Street* and *"Woman Hollering Creek" and Other Stories*, is often compared to poetry—or even identified *as* poetry. The two books will be treated in the following pages as fiction; yet, like the best of poetry, these books can bring new discoveries, insights, and surprises with each rereading.

INTRODUCTION TO CISNEROS' WORK

Introduction

The House on Mango Street and *"Woman Hollering Creek" and Other Stories* have enjoyed wide critical and popular favor, and deservedly so. Engagingly readable, their appeal is immediate, yet they open up areas of experience new to many U.S. readers. Sandra Cisneros' fictional "voice" and her feminism are often praised, yet there are many voices in her fiction—not all of them female—and each is wholly individual, defining a character we recognize as a unique human being, often in only a few sentences. Academic critics point out mythic connections in Cisneros' stories, yet in each of them—whether the setting is Chicago in the 1960s, 1980s San Antonio, or early-twentieth-century Mexico— the real world is foremost, crowding into our senses by way of language that is concrete and precise.

The House on Mango Street

The first of these works, *The House on Mango Street*, originally published in 1984, has been especially popular in schools. The narrator and main character is Esperanza Cordero, a girl just entering adolescence, who introduces and describes her family and friends and her day-to-day life with all its troubles and pleasures, in a direct, engaging, and delightfully original voice. Esperanza speaks to readers her own age in their own language; older readers will gain from her narrative an ironic awareness that Esperanza herself does not yet possess.

The book has been called a collection of stories, even a group of prose poems. Yet if a novel is a longish fiction following the course of ordinary life and showing the development of a character through tension and conflict, *Mango Street* fits the definition very comfortably. Its central theme is a universal one: a young girl's struggle both to find her own place within her culture and, at the same time, to discover and preserve her individuality. The book's structure, which may appear at first to be a random ordering of incidents and reflections, is actually what holds the seemingly disparate pieces of narrative together, creating lines of tension and conflict out of what Esperanza tells us.

"Woman Hollering Creek" and Other Stories

"Woman Hollering Creek" and Other Stories, the second of Cisneros' fictional works, *is* a group of 22 short pieces, all self-contained, variously

set in Texas, Chicago, and Mexico, mostly from the 1960s to the late 1980s (with one exception, "Eyes of Zapata," which takes place in the early years of the twentieth century).

Cisneros' Writing Style

Both *The House on Mango Street* and *"Woman Hollering Creek" and Other Stories* by Cisneros may seem to the hasty first-time reader to be casually, even loosely constructed, yet the careful reader suspects that nothing could be further from the truth. The poet W. B. Yeats writes, about writing: "A line may take us hours maybe; / Yet if it does not seem a moment's thought, / Our stitching and unstitching has been naught." The "stitching and unstitching" Yeats meant was the writing of poetry, the painstaking effort to make it look effortless. Cisneros' fiction may sometimes "seem a moment's thought," but she is a fooler. Like the best poetry, her work is both direct and ambiguous; it rings true on many levels. It challenges and continues to reward the serious reader.

Brief Synopses

The House on Mango Street

Esperanza Cordero and her parents, sister, and brothers move into a house on Mango Street, after having lived in numerous other locations in Chicago, only some of which Esperanza remembers. At least this latest house is the Corderos' own, but in other respects, it is not the house Esperanza would have hoped for. Esperanza meets some of her neighbors—Cathy (whose family is about to move out because the neighborhood is going downhill), Lucy and Rachel (two sisters who live across the street), a boy named Tito, another named Meme Ortiz (whose family has moved into Cathy's house), yet another boy named Louie, Louie's cousin Marin, and Louie's other cousin.

Esperanza gets to know Marin a little better and learns that she is hoping to marry a boy in Puerto Rico but that she is still interested in other boys. Esperanza reflects that people who don't live in the neighborhood are afraid to come into it, whereas those who live there feel quite safe but are afraid to go into *other* neighborhoods. She tells about the Vargas kids, whose father left and whose mother can't control them, and about Alicia, who is going to the university and at the same time keeping house for her father. Esperanza and her friends hang out, looking at clouds, talking idly. A woman gives Esperanza, Lucy, and Rachel three pairs of high-heeled shoes, which they wear around the neighborhood.

Esperanza pleads with her mother to let her take her lunch to school, but when she is allowed to do so, she doesn't enjoy it. She goes to a baptismal party for a baby cousin and dances with her uncle. She, Nenny, Lucy, and Rachel talk about getting hips, and Esperanza gets her first job, in a photo-developing store. Her grandfather dies in Mexico, her Aunt Lupe dies in Chicago, and Esperanza goes to a fortune-teller who informs her that she will have a home in the heart. At a dance, her friend Marin meets a man who is later injured in a hit-and-run accident; Marin waits in the hospital while he dies. Esperanza describes two neighborhood adults whom she finds interesting: Edna's daughter Ruthie and a jukebox repairman named Earl. She tells about a boy—Sire—who sometimes stares at her, and talks about her relationship to four trees growing from the sidewalk in front of her house.

Then Esperanza describes two married women she knows— *Mamacita*, who is very fat, very homesick, and cannot speak English, and Rafaela, who is young and beautiful, and whose husband locks her in their apartment while he goes out to play dominoes with his friends. Sally, who is about Esperanza's age, makes herself attractive to boys and young men but is mistreated by her father, who is afraid she will run away with some boy or young man. And Minerva (who also writes poems), not much older than Esperanza, has two little children and a husband who leaves her sometimes but then comes back and beats her.

When she has a house, Esperanza says, it will be a big, fine one, and she will let "bums" stay upstairs in the attic. She has decided to be independent, like a man. Her mother tells her that she herself quit school because she was ashamed of her clothes.

Sally's father beats her so badly that her mother allows her to come and stay with Esperanza's family, but he comes to get her, begs her to come home with him, and then beats her worse. Esperanza and Sally go to play in an overgrown and deserted garden, but Sally would rather hang out with the boys, and Esperanza embarrasses herself by trying to protect Sally, who doesn't want to be protected. The two girls go to a carnival, and Sally leaves with a boy; Esperanza, waiting for her to return, is overpowered by several strangers and sexually assaulted by one of them.

Now Sally has married a young man she met at a school function, and he makes her stay in their house and won't let her friends visit. Lucy and Rachel's youngest sister, an infant, dies; at their house, Esperanza meets her friends' three aunts (or, most likely, great aunts), who draw her aside and tell her she is special. When she leaves Mango Street, they say, she must not neglect to come back for those who can't leave. Her friend Alicia echoes this advice when they talk on Edna's steps. And, at last, Esperanza says that she *will* have a house of her own, she *will* someday leave Mango Street—and, sometimes, writing about it helps her make *it* leave *her*—but she will come back for the others.

"Woman Hollering Creek" and Other Stories

Twenty-two short pieces, all self-contained, variously set in Texas, Chicago, and Mexico, mostly from the 1960s to the late 1980s (with one exception, "Eyes of Zapata," which takes place in the early years of the twentieth century) comprise *"Woman Hollering Creek" and Other Stories.* Characters narrate all but three or four of the stories, and these voices vary from that of a five-or- six-year-old girl to that of an elderly man. Several of the pieces are only a page or two long; the two longest, "Eyes of Zapata" and *"Bien* Pretty," are each about 29 pages. Most of the stories are non-traditional in structure, following a non-linear shape in which the narrator "circles" around her or his topic, examining it from various angles and in various times. Those that do follow a conventionally linear pattern tend to flatten that pattern ironically. All of the pieces are serious; many are very funny, too.

List of Characters

From *The House on Mango Street*

Esperanza Cordero The narrator and central character.

Nenny (Magdalena) Esperanza's younger sister.

Papa, Mama, Carlos and Kiki Esperanza's parents (Mr. and Mrs. E. Cordero) and her two younger brothers.

Cathy A neighbor girl.

Edna The woman who owns and lives in the apartment building next door; the mother of Ruthie, a childlike woman.

Lucy and Rachel Two girls who live across the street; Lucy is the older sister, Rachel the younger.

Meme Ortiz The boy who moves into Cathy's house.

Marin A neighborhood girl, older than Esperanza.

The Vargas family Rosa and her children, who are many and out of control.

Alicia One of Esperanza's neighbors; Alicia is a university student and becomes a friend to Esperanza.

Darius A neighborhood boy.

Sister Superior Esperanza's school principal.

Aunt Lupe (Guadalupe) One of Esperanza's aunts.

Elenita A witch woman.

Geraldo A man Marin meets at a dance.

Earl   A man who lives in Edna's basement apartment.

Sire   A boy Esperanza is attracted to.

Mamacita   A woman who never leaves her apartment.

Rafaela   Another married neighborhood woman.

Sally   A friend of Esperanza's.

Minerva   A young woman whose husband beats her.

The three sisters   Lucy and Rachel's great-aunts.

From "Woman Hollering Creek" and Other Stories

Lucy Anguiano   A little girl in Texas (in "My Lucy Friend . . .").

Rachel   The girl who narrates "Eleven," on her eleventh birthday.

Salvador   A small boy (in "Salvador Late or Early") who cares for his younger brothers.

Micaela   The narrator of "'Mericans," and possibly also of "Tepeyac"; she is a girl of about 11 in the first of these two stories and shifts between approximately that age and adulthood in the second.

"Chaq Uxmal Paloquín" (a.k.a. Boy Baby, a.k.a. Chato)   The man beloved of the narrator in "One Holy Night."

"Ixchel"   The narrator of "One Holy Night," who is given this name by her beloved; she is not called by any other name in the story. Both "Chaq" and "Ixchel" are the names of figures in Maya myth.

Patricia Bernadette Benavídez   A San Antonio teenager who disappears and then reappears, the *tocaya* of Patricia Chávez, who is the narrator of "My *Tocaya*."

Cleófilas   A young Mexican woman who marries a *tejano*, Juan Pedro, and then begins to regret her choice (in "Woman Hollering Creek").

Graciela and Felice   Two Texas women who help Cleófilas.

Tristán (a.k.a. Rudy Cantú)   A dancer (in "Remember the Alamo").

Clemencia   An artist in Texas, whose mother told her "Never Marry a Mexican."

Inés   Wife of Emiliano Zapata, the Mexican patriot and revolutionary leader; she narrates "Eyes of Zapata." (Inés is a fictional character based on a historical woman.)

Rosario (Chayo) De Leon   A university student who leaves the cut-off braid of her hair as an offering of thanks to the Virgin of Guadalupe (in "Little Miracles, Kept Promises").

Flavio Munguía (a.k.a. "Rogelio Velasco")   The lover of Lupe, who narrates "*Bien* Pretty"; he is the "writer" of "Tin Tan Tan."

Lupe   The narrator of "*Bien* Pretty"; she is an artist who has moved from San Francisco to San Antonio.

> **Note:** Other characters in "*Woman Hollering Creek" and Other Stories* are important but unnamed; these include the children who narrate "My Lucy Friend Who Smells Like Corn," "Mexican Movies," and "Barbie-Q"; the female narrator of "Anguiano Religious Articles" and the male speaker in "*Los* Boxers"; and the two women whose conversation forms the story "The Marlboro Man."

Character Map: *The House on Mango Street*

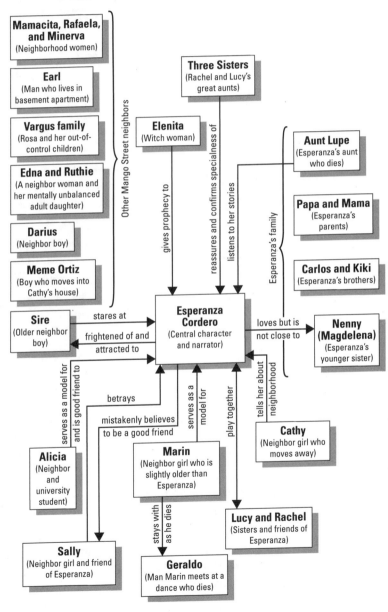

Mamacita, Rafaela, and Minerva
(Neighborhood women)

Earl
(Man who lives in basement apartment)

Vargus family
(Rosa and her out-of-control children)

Edna and Ruthie
(A neighbor woman and her mentally unbalanced adult daughter)

Darius
(Neighbor boy)

Meme Ortiz
(Boy who moves into Cathy's house)

Other Mango Street neighbors

Three Sisters
(Rachel and Lucy's great aunts)

Elenita
(Witch woman)

gives prophecy to

reassures and confirms specialness of

listens to her stories

Aunt Lupe
(Esperanza's aunt who dies)

Papa and Mama
(Esperanza's parents)

Esperanza's family

Carlos and Kiki
(Esperanza's brothers)

Sire
(Older neighbor boy)

stares at

frightened of and attracted to

Esperanza Cordero
(Central character and narrator)

loves but is not close to

Nenny (Magdelena)
(Esperanza's younger sister)

serves as a model for and is good friend to

betrays

mistakenly believes to be a good friend

serves as a model for

play together

tells her about neighborhood

Cathy
(Neighbor girl who moves away)

Alicia
(Neighbor and university student)

Marin
(Neighbor girl who is slightly older than Esperanza)

Lucy and Rachel
(Sisters and friends of Esperanza)

stays with as he dies

Sally
(Neighbor girl and friend of Esperanza)

Geraldo
(Man Marin meets at a dance who dies)

CRITICAL COMMENTARIES: *THE HOUSE ON MANGO STREET*

Part One

The House on Mango Street; Hairs; Boys & Girls; My Name

Summary

Note: The House on Mango Street is divided into 44 separately titled sections averaging about two-and-one-half pages each. Each of these sections might stand alone; together they work as a novel. These critical commentaries refer to the sections as "chapters" and consider them in numbered groups for the sake of convenience.

In the first chapter, the speaker reveals a little about her family and her life. She talks about the house she lives in and about some of the other places she has lived. The family has moved numerous times and, at the same time, has been growing, until now there are four children: the speaker has two brothers (Carlos and Kiki) and one sister (Nenny), besides her two parents. The speaker was ashamed of the last place they lived. This new house is small, with crumbling bricks, small windows, a small backyard, and no front yard, but it has three bedrooms and the speaker's parents own it.

In "Hairs," the speaker describes how everyone in her family has different kinds of hair, and how her mother's hair smells comfortably like bread before it's baked.

Carlos and Kiki, the two boys, play together outside but can't be seen talking to girls, the speaker tells us in "Boys & Girls." She herself has to watch out that her sister doesn't get into trouble, but Nenny is not the "best friend" she wants or would choose. Someday, though, she will have a best friend.

Then, in "My Name," she tells us who she is: Esperanza, which in English translates to *hope*; it was also the name of her great-grandmother, a strong woman who suffered because her culture did not like strong women. Esperanza doesn't like her name, but at least it is better than her sister's—Magdalena—and sounds better in Spanish than in English. But her sister's name has a nickname—Nenny—whereas her own does not.

Commentary

The first four chapters have little or no plot action and minimal—although valuable—exposition: We learn the names of the speaker and her siblings and something about their ages and birth order (Kiki is the youngest of the four, he and Carlos are "best friends"—so it's a safe guess that Carlos, too, is younger than Esperanza—and Nenny is younger as well, so Esperanza must be the eldest). We learn something about the family's ethnicity and socio-economic status. But most of what happens in these first four chapters is our introduction to Esperanza.

As the narrator, Esperanza speaks to her audience (the reader) with a total absence of self-consciousness. To whom is Esperanza speaking/ writing? Although sometimes she records feelings and impressions in a manner that suggests a private journal or diary, more often she includes *information* that a diarist (especially a child) would probably deem unnecessary. She will occasionally address other characters directly, but for the most part, what she says and the way she says it suggests that the hearer/reader she has in mind is someone like herself, a girl her own age who does not know her but who understands what she is saying because the two are *simpático*. In other words, she seems consciously or unconsciously to be addressing the "best friend" she has not yet met.

What Esperanza tells directly about herself here is relatively little; what she tells *in*directly is a good deal more informative. First of all, she is at this point a child, although in certain ways, she is older than her years. She still gets in bed with her parents for comfort; she enumerates small differences among family members that prove each is an individual. Part of her self-identity is as an older sister. She feels responsible for guiding Nenny, although there is a lack of sympathy between her and her sister.

Esperanza is also childish in what she selects to tell: not her parents' names, for example, but only Papa and Mama; not their occupations (something only adults consider important), but how their hair looks. Her disappointment in the "new" house is childish; she tells us very little about it but does not hide her resentment that it is not something better. She is naïve enough to have hoped for her parents' dream house and childish enough to reveal her disappointment, despite her realization that this is probably not just a temporary move for the family and her attempt to sound sophisticated about that realization.

In at least one way, however, Esperanza is already the woman she will become. She values her strength and her independence (her identification with her great-grandmother); she is someone who makes her own decisions and refuses to be a follower (unlike Nenny, who will become just like the Vargas kids if allowed to play with them). Even the fact that she volunteers very little about herself is indicative of her independence: She keeps her own counsel. Esperanza sees herself as somewhat mysterious. If she could, she would re-baptize herself as "something like Zeze the X," someone unusual, exotic—and masked.

As readers, we should remember that Esperanza's real name (chosen by her parents, fictionally, but chosen by Cisneros actually) has value not only as a device for revealing what this protagonist doesn't like: the sad, old-fashioned Mexican associations it has for her; its passive, "feminine" sound (unlike "Zeze the X"); its harsh consonants when spoken in English; the impossibility of its being shortened into a nickname. Translated into English, Esperanza tells us, her name means "hope," and of course that is basically what it means. But it shares its Latin root with the English words "spirit" and "aspiration" (something more than mere "hope": ambition, daring, strong desire), both of which, like the Spanish word "*esperanza*," derive from a word meaning *breath*. The spirit that animates this protagonist is what distinguishes her. Until she has a "best friend," she says (meaning, until she is able to choose a friend, as she cannot choose her family, for being a child is by definition being unable to choose), she will be like a balloon on a tether, unable to rise with the spirit that fills her.

Glossary

(Here and in the following glossary sections, difficult words and phrases, as well as allusions and historical references, are explained.)

Year of the Horse   Chinese designation of a specific year within a 12-year cycle, used (like sun signs in Western astrological lore) to predict things about people born in those years. This pinpoints Esperanza's birth year as 1954.

Lisandra A feminine variation of Alessandro (Alexander); Esperanza's choice here is arguably "stronger" than the name her parents gave her, derived from a Greek name meaning literally "defender of men"; it is also suggestive of Alexander the Great (356–323 B.C.), a famous Macedonian king and military conquerer. Also, like Magdalena (which can be shortened to "Nenny"), but unlike Esperanza, Lisandra can be shortened to a nickname—Sandy or Sandra.

Part Two

Cathy Queen of Cats; Our Good Day; Laughter; Gil's Furniture Bought & Sold; Meme Ortiz; Louie, His Cousin & His Other Cousin

Summary

A girl named Cathy, one of Esperanza's neighbors, tells Esperanza about the neighborhood. She says she'll be Esperanza's friend for a few days, but then her family is moving. Cathy says she's related to the Queen of France, and someday her family will inherit some property, but for now they have to move because the neighborhood is going downhill.

Cathy has warned Esperanza about the two girls across the street, but in "Our Good Day" Esperanza decides to be their friend anyway. She gives the two girls (Lucy and Rachel) some money because they are all going in together to buy a bicycle from a neighborhood boy. Cathy leaves, and Esperanza, Lucy, and Rachel take a ride on their new, wobbly bicycle.

In "Laughter," Esperanza says she and Nenny don't look alike, but that there are likenesses between them deeper than looks.

The girls visit a neighborhood second-hand store ("Gil's Furniture . . ."). Nenny asks the owner about a music box, and he opens the lid and lets them listen. Nenny asks how much it costs, but the storeowner says it's not for sale.

Cathy has moved, and a boy called Meme Ortiz moves into her house. There's a backyard with a large tree in it. The children hold the First Annual Tarzan Jumping Contest in this tree, and Meme wins, breaking both arms.

Downstairs from Meme's family, a Puerto Rican family has moved in, including Esperanza's brother's friend Louie and two cousins, one of whom is an older girl named Marin who spends all day indoors, babysitting Louie's little sisters. Esperanza knows Marin wears heavy makeup and dark hose. Louie's other cousin, an older boy, comes by one day in a Cadillac and takes everyone for a ride. When a police car follows them, Louie's cousin makes everyone get out, crashes the Cadillac, and is arrested.

Commentary

In these chapters, we get to know Esperanza a little better, and we feel her relax a bit, allowing her language to become slightly more informal and at the same time more colorful.

How old is Esperanza? About a year later, she will imply that she is about to enter the eighth grade, so we may guess that she is now eleven or twelve. But (as another Cisneros protagonist will remind us) "eleven" contains ten, and nine—and three, for that matter; each "age" remains within the person, layered over with the added years like the inside of an onion. In these chapters, "ten" or even "nine" seems to predominate in Esperanza, who rides triple on a bike and jumps through (or from?) a tree.

As everyone who has ever been eleven or twelve ought to remember, no one moves suddenly and irrevocably into adulthood or even adolescence—nor is the move a smoothly gradual one. Throughout *Mango Street*, Esperanza provides a superb illustration of this sometimes-uncomfortable truth: Sometimes she seems to look backward into childhood, sometimes forward into womanhood. Part of the reason for her looking backward, in this group of chapters, is that she has become acquainted with some neighborhood children, most of whom seem to be younger than she. Socialization seems to be easy for Esperanza, and she naturally gravitates into the familiar relationships and activities of childhood. She accepts Cathy as a short-term "friend" but quickly changes this allegiance, which means little to her, for another "friendship" with Lucy and Rachel (who tells Esperanza that for five dollars she'll be her friend forever); she knows none of these is the "best friend" she has wished to have. Esperanza is not the kind of girl who hangs out with younger children so she can boss them around, but she and Lucy both have younger sisters whom they cannot ignore, and there seems to be only one older girl in the neighborhood—Marin, about whose name Esperanza is not even sure at first, and whose makeup and dark hose signify that she has already made the short crossing out of childhood.

Literary Device

But despite being part of a younger crowd, Esperanza is still an independent individual. She takes Nenny's savings without permission (high-handedly; she's the older sister and guesses—apparently correctly—that Nenny will be glad to own a share of the $15 bicycle). Within a few seconds of meeting Lucy and Rachel, she corrects Lucy's grammar and is amused to find that Lucy doesn't even recognize the correction. Esperanza's individuality is best expressed, however, in her gift for metaphor. Her descriptions are peppered with similes and other figures that are spontaneous, unforced, entirely apt—and entirely in character for an 11-year-old (for example, after running into a lamp-post, a Cadillac's "nose" is "all pleated like an alligator's"). This is who Esperanza *is*. She sees things in her own way.

Theme

This difference between Esperanza and the others, in fact, is the beginning of the tension that becomes part of *Mango Street*'s central theme. A unique individual, potentially a "strong woman" like her great-grandmother (who was punished for her strength), Esperanza still gets along easily and well with other children. But when she and Nenny go into the "junk store" and Nenny asks about a music box, we see a reaction that clearly separates Esperanza from Nenny—and from anything she herself has previously felt, so that she is as surprised at herself as at the incident that caused her to react. Esperanza's own reaction baffles her, and she calls it "stupid." In fact, it is a response to real beauty encountered unexpectedly. Nenny reaches for money; Esperanza knows, before the storeowner has said it, that such magic is not for sale. The difference between Esperanza and her sister is implied: It is a difference of worlds, the mundane world of prettiness and cost, and the spiritual world of beauty and worth. As the book progresses, Esperanza will be torn between these two worlds.

Glossary

marimbas   plural of *marimba*, a musical instrument resembling the xylophone.

"Meme"   Meme Ortiz's nickname seems to be derived from a Spanish word—*"memo"*—meaning a stupid person or a fool, or perhaps from *"memez,"* stupidity.

"she wears dark nylons...."   style of dress and makeup that would have been considered sexually provocative.

Part Three

Marin; Those Who Don't; There Was an Old Woman She Had So Many Children She Didn't Know What to Do; Alicia Who Sees Mice

Summary

In "Marin," Louie's girl cousin Marin hangs out with the younger girls after her aunt gets home; she smokes cigarettes, wears short skirts, and flirts with boys. Marin says she's going to marry her boyfriend who's still in Puerto Rico, but since he doesn't have a job, she's saving her money. Louie's parents, however, have written to Marin's parents, saying they're sending her back to Puerto Rico.

In "Those Who Don't," Esperanza says people who don't live in their neighborhood are afraid to come into it, but the ones who live there know who everyone is and are not afraid. Everyone there is brown. They are, however, afraid to go into neighborhoods where the people are another color.

"There Was an Old Woman She Had So Many Children She Didn't Know What to Do" is about the Vargas family, in which there are so many children that the mother, Rosa Vargas, can't control them. Every day she weeps because her husband left her with all these children. They are bad, says Esperanza, with no respect for anyone. They take terrible chances with themselves, and people in the neighborhood are so used to this that they have stopped trying to keep the Vargas children out of trouble.

Alicia is a neighbor Esperanza first heard about from Cathy the Cat Queen. Alicia is an older girl who goes to college and takes care of her widowed father. He thinks a woman's place is in the kitchen, making tortillas, but Alicia commutes across town to the university because she doesn't want to work all her life in a factory or at home making tortillas.

Commentary

This group of chapters begins with Louie's cousin Marin and ends with Alicia. Although Marin will all but disappear from the book after our introduction to her, she and Alicia—and Rosa Vargas—are important in that they are all older than Esperanza, all potential "role models" because they are women she knows, female participants in her culture, at a time when she has begun to turn away from her own mother and female relatives and to look elsewhere for clues about who she will be. Marin, although in fact still a child in many ways, has entered the world of womanhood before Esperanza and has become one of the younger girl's guides. As such, although Esperanza's parents would certainly do their best to discourage such a development, Marin represents a very real possibility for Esperanza's future.

Before the 1970s, many working-class girls, urban and rural, stopped attending school after the eighth grade. Abortion was illegal, bearing a child out of wedlock was considered shameful, and young women frequently married at 14 or 15; a 13-year-old bride was not unheard of, especially in communities where many parents and grandparents were immigrants to the U.S. from places where an educated woman was something of a curiosity in any but the wealthiest classes. Given this, Marin must be very young indeed to want to conceal her marriage plans from her family: perhaps a year older than Esperanza, 12-going-on-13 and physically mature for her age; or perhaps two years older than Esperanza and emotionally younger than her age-mates. In any case, Marin's family in Puerto Rico has sent her to live with an aunt in the U.S. for some reason, and now the aunt's family says she's "too much trouble"—despite the fact that she baby-sits while her aunt works—and wants to send her back. That trouble sounds like boy trouble, probably the same kind of boy trouble that got Marin sent to live with her aunt in the first place. Her family, fearing an unwanted pregnancy, separated her from her jobless boyfriend; now her aunt would like to get Marin off her hands in the same condition she arrived in. And Marin is a boy-crazy girl.

Readers born after 1960 or so can probably not appreciate the deft accuracy with which Cisneros has sketched Marin's character and the rueful poignancy of the sketch nearly so well as those who grew up when Marin was growing up. The so-called "sexual revolution" was, in the mid-1960s, still a phrase rather than a reality, especially for Catholic girls in Latino families. An unmarried girl who became pregnant ("got in trouble" was the phrase in English) and could not be married immediately was, if possible, sent to far-off relatives to have her baby. Young women were expected to be virgins on their wedding day, and many of them were. A great many young teenage girls who knew how babies were born—frequently because their mothers and married sisters gave birth at home—had only the haziest notion of how they were conceived. Marin, whatever the level or accuracy of her knowledge in this regard, has at least shared it with Esperanza and Lucy, who at 11 or so have probably been entirely ignorant. And Marin herself is likely to be almost as ignorant. Although she presents herself as a sexual object, it is not really sex Marin is interested in—it is love. She dreams of romance, of a stranger met, perhaps on a train, who will "take [her] to live in a big house far away."

Character Insight

Readers who have grown up seeing sex presented frankly *as* sex on television and movie screens, who find nothing remarkable, much less shameful, in the fact of never-married mothers raising their children alone, who have always lived in a culture with easy access to effective contraceptives and legal abortion, are apt to misunderstand or misinterpret Marin's combination of brazen (for her time) sexual invitation and innocent romanticism. Marin is neither stupid nor perverse, only naïve. In her culture (especially in her Latino culture, but in a larger sense simply in the United States of the 1950s and 1960s), girls were protected from sexual knowledge.

In the lyrics of popular songs, in movies and on television, sex was presented as "love," and love was, in most cases, inseparable from marriage. Young men were expected to be more knowing than young women, and one of the things they knew was to couch their sexual overtures in terms both non-specific and romantic. Thus, when boys say absurd things about loving her eyes, Marin *knows* that they are talking about sex, and she is curious about it, but the subject itself remains disguised and hazy. She is free to fantasize about a handsome stranger who will buy her nice things and pay her incessant compliments, carry her away to a lovely house with furniture just as she wants it, everything her own. In the evening, he will come home and kiss her passionately, and it will all be like a movie scene with rapturous music playing as the couple embraces and the screen fades out.

A handsome stranger, 15 or 16 years earlier, carried away Rosa Vargas; instead of fading out, however, her screen went to diaper pails and one baby a year until her husband left her with no money and no explanation. Rosa's situation is not unusual. Given the ingredients of early marriage, unreasonable (and conflicting) expectations, strict religious laws against contraception, and never enough money, the wonder is that her situation was not even more common (as indeed it was to become in subsequent decades). Thus Rosa's children grow up without parental or cultural guidance, without the care even of the neighborhood, whose concerned adults they spit upon, and "without respect for all things living, including themselves," as Esperanza wisely says. Thus "Rosa's Eddie V." stands with his pals, looking threatening to strangers (people of "another color" who venture into the neighborhood, usually by mistake, Esperanza thinks), while her Angel dives off roofs. And thus Esperanza sees, along with the interesting and exciting example of young womanhood presented by Marin and her admirers, the other side of the same coin as presented by Rosa Vargas. Marin sees it too, of course, but has not yet understood it, perhaps because she doesn't want to.

There is another alternative—one that is for Esperanza in the middle 1960s still daring and unusual. Her neighbor Alicia has a difficult life, not of course as hard (because not hopeless) as Rosa's, but nowhere near as glamorous from a young girl's point of view as the life Marin expects and dreams about. Alicia is trying to span two worlds: the traditional one her mother inhabited, where a woman's place is in the kitchen making tortillas, and the world of education, infrequently inhabited by working-class Latino women in the 1960s.

Theme

Every day, Alicia takes a long commute to a university where, even if she is studying a traditionally "female" subject like nursing or elementary education, she is likely to face prejudice from teachers and classmates on account of her ethnicity; if she is studying anything else, she must battle sexism as well. Every evening—after she has shopped and prepared an evening meal and done the laundry and other housework—she must study in an atmosphere dominated by the father who thinks she is foolish or worse to want to go to college. Then she must get up early to fix breakfast and lunch for her father before starting all over again. Esperanza sees Alicia's difficulties; are the rewards of her life as apparent? This is part of the tension that Esperanza will feel throughout the period of this book. And while it is easy for an adult to say that Esperanza's choice is obvious, we should remember that—

to a young girl entering adolescence—Marin's imaginary rewards seem much simpler, more exciting, and more immediate than Alicia's distant and uncertain ones.

A note is in order on Esperanza's assessment of her neighborhood in "Those Who Don't." Some readers might infer that Cisneros is painting too rosy a picture of these urban streets, when she has Esperanza say that those who live there are not afraid of what might happen to them in their own neighborhood. In fact, Esperanza seems to see most of what goes on around her and knows there is safety for children in numbers. Her perception of her neighborhood as a basically safe place for its inhabitants is correct: In the mid-1960s, guns are relatively scarce, and the high-powered weapons that will appear in later decades are still far in the future. There is indeed drug use: Alcohol and marijuana are relatively common, heroin less so (and heroin users are dangerous mostly to themselves), but cocaine in powder form is only beginning to reappear as a street drug after many decades, and crack cocaine is still unheard of. There are indeed street gangs, but these are not as dominant as they will become in later years. The Vargas kids, who respect nothing and no one, are still in training for their lives of crime, should they survive so long; the rest of the people in the neighborhood—whose Latino culture includes a strong, traditional code of honor and respect for family—look out for each other. Esperanza is probably sheltered by her family (as Sandra Cisneros has said she was sheltered by hers), but basically she is right: Stifling as her neighborhood can be to a young woman's potential, she is about as safe there as any girl in any neighborhood has ever been.

Part Four

Darius and the Clouds; And Some More; The Family of Little Feet; A Rice Sandwich; Chanclas

Summary

In "Darius and the Clouds," Esperanza says that the sky is important; there is not enough of it where she lives, but she and her friends make do with what they have. A boy named Darius points to a cloud and says it is God.

In "And Some More," Esperanza, her friends Lucy and Rachel, and her sister Nenny are talking idly, watching the clouds, and Esperanza makes some comments about things she's read. The girls start trading insults, and one thing leads to another until Esperanza tells the neighbor girls to get out of her yard, and they say they'll never come back again. Nobody leaves, however, and the insults continue while Nenny, pointing to clouds, calls them by names—human names, that is.

"The Family of Little Feet" starts out as a story Esperanza is telling about a family whose members are small people with little feet. One day the mother comes out with a paper bag full of high-heeled shoes that she gives to Esperanza, Rachel, and Lucy. The girls put the shoes on and walk around the neighborhood. The shoes have a strange effect on people: Benny, the store man, tells the girls they are too young to be wearing shoes like that and threatens to call the police on them. A boy riding by on a bicycle flirts with them. A drunk near a tavern tries to make conversation, and Rachel tells him her name, but Esperanza and Lucy make her leave when the drunk offers her a dollar for a kiss. They take the shoes home and take them off, and when Lucy and Rachel's mother throws them away a few days later, the girls don't care.

In "A Rice Sandwich," Esperanza comes home for lunch every day, and she decides she wants to take her lunch and eat at school. Her mother says she doesn't need to; Esperanza begs and pleads and eventually wears her mother down. But when the time comes, she has to take her mother's letter of permission to the principal (Sister Superior), who knows she doesn't live far enough away to justify bringing her lunch to school. She makes Esperanza point out her house from the window, and Esperanza begins to cry. Then the nun says she may stay that day, but not again. Esperanza goes to the canteen and eats her sandwich, crying as the other children watch.

In "Chanclas," Esperanza and her mother are going to her baby cousin's baptism party in the church basement. Her mother gets new clothes for Esperanza, but forgets shoes, so she has to wear her school shoes. This embarrasses her, and while everyone else dances, she sits in a folding chair and won't get up. Finally her uncle drags her out on the floor and dances with her, and they are so good that everyone watches and applauds. Her mother is proud of her, and a boy Esperanza knows watches her dance.

Commentary

In this group of chapters, Esperanza—aided and abetted in some instances by her friends—gives way first of all to silliness. With other children, she stares at clouds and finds significant shapes in them. Later, with Nenny, Lucy, and Rachel, she again considers the clouds, an exercise that ends up in a silly session as the girls "play the dozens" on each other. Pals again later, they prance around in high heels—an escapade that Esperanza introduces with a silly once-upon-a-time story about little people with little feet. Then Esperanza makes such a foolish fuss—for days—about taking her lunch to school that her mother at last gives in. The silliness of "*Chanclas*" is almost anticlimactic, with Esperanza pouting in a folding chair while everyone else dances, because she has had to wear her school shoes to the party.

All of this silliness is part of early adolescence; no one can act—or feel—quite so childish as someone who is about to leave childhood. Here Esperanza almost revels in it, from her sly embedded rhyme about "Darius, who doesn't like school, who is sometimes stupid and mostly a fool" (33) to her story about the "little feet" to her list of reasons why she should be allowed to take her lunch to school. At other times, being silly involves feeling tremendously miserable about how silly one knows one is being, and then (if one is a girl and crying is allowed) bursting into tears about it, which is sort of the frosting on the cake of silliness. But the silliness of these chapters contains the seeds of other kinds of things: spirituality, imagination, humility, and above all self-realization—the beginnings of growth out of childhood.

Literary
Device

The business of looking at clouds is an example. Very young children can learn to look at these shifting shapes and see doggies, bunny rabbits, and the like; Darius sees God—and who knows what this may mean to Darius, but to Esperanza it is a *wise* vision. Why? Esperanza knows this cloud isn't literally the creator of the universe, so she knows what Darius says is a metaphor of some kind, one of those metaphors that one *feels* to be right even when it seems to defy reason. (It is probably, to be technical, an instance of *synecdoche*, that is, the part substituted for the whole, a more mundane example of which might be Lucy's dialectal introduction of herself earlier in the book: "Me, I'm Texas.")

However much Esperanza has thought about God—and she says nothing more on the subject—she has learned in her Catholic schools that God is everywhere and invisible but can also be in one specific place and time, as in the consecrated host. She has learned that God can be *incarnate*, as in the human body of Christ. As a child and a poet, she knows in her bones the mythic truth that the gods have always manifested themselves in natural phenomena. She also knows in her heart, whether or not she has read William Blake's poem "Auguries of Innocence," that one of the gifts of childhood is to be able "To see a world in a grain of sand / And heaven in a wild flower, / Hold infinity in the palm of your hand / And eternity in an hour." There are few grains of sand and scarcely any wild flowers in Esperanza's neighborhood, but as she says, they make the best of what they have, including the necessary sky, and Esperanza's romantic, poetic heart recognizes what Darius says as important and true.

Character
Insight

Clouds, too, are personally important to Esperanza, probably because they are light, buoyant, airy. The image of a cloud floating free, evolving at its own whim, in plain sight but mysterious, is attractive to this girl who feels like a tethered balloon wishing for release. Esperanza has done some reading up on clouds, between Darius's observation (when she describes some clouds as "the kind like pillows") and her next opportunity for educating her sister and friends, who do not react well to her erudition, with Nenny mocking her by "naming" each individual cloud with the name of a person, and Lucy turning on

Esperanza with a comment about her ugly face. Despite this, however, Esperanza's identity now takes on a new dimension: She is the one who knows the names and reasons for things and uses her reading to bolster her older-sister authority and her maturing sense of who she is.

Esperanza matures in other directions as well in these chapters. Because "the canteen" sounds glamorous, she insists on taking her sandwich to school so she can eat there. But her mother's note makes it fairly plain to the Sister Superior what's going on, and Esperanza is defeated. She tries to justify her tears by implying she was insulted and/or intimidated, but neither of these explanations will stand up to much scrutiny. In fact, she feels foolish, and when she discovers that "the canteen" is "nothing special" and her sandwich cold and greasy, she has effectively learned an adult fact of life: You can't always get what you want, but sometimes when you *do* get it, it isn't what you wanted after all. Similarly, in "Chanclas," Esperanza learns to put things in perspective, as her feet go back to normal size after having swelled, with her own concentration on them, completely out of proportion. And in "The Family of Little Feet," all three girls come to a tacit understanding and agreement that they are not ready quite yet for the kinds of attention they attract when they dress like grown-up women.

Literary Device

But they are practicing, edging closer to the border of that country where to be a woman means being "beautiful"—attractive to men, with one's walk hobbled and the shape of one's legs and buttocks exaggerated by wearing high-heeled shoes. And Rachel's encounter with the drunk is an uncomfortable foreshadowing of the disaster that awaits Esperanza. At the same time, however, Esperanza has noticed that her boy cousin at the baptism party, whom she apparently finds attractive, watches her appreciatively as she dances, even though she is *not* wearing sexy shoes.

Glossary

frijoles   cooked beans; refried beans.

salamander   a limbed, tailed amphibian with a soft, moist skin.

double-dutch   or "double Dutch"; a children's game of jump rope in which two turners swing two ropes simultaneously in a crisscross pattern for the person jumping.

300 Spartans   an American movie made in the 1950s about the Battle of Thermopylae (in the Persian War) where, in 480 B.C., a Persian army commanded by Xerxes destroyed a Spartan army led by Leonidas. The Spartans, who held the pass against tremendous odds, became an exemplum of bravery and physical courage.

chanclas   (Spanish) plural of *chancla*, a type of open shoe.

"that boy who is my cousin by first communion or something el" nonsense; "first communion" is what Catholics call the occasion on which a person first receives the sacrament of the Eucharist, usually as a child of about seven, so Esperanza is probably searching for a phrase here ("first cousin once removed," perhaps) and coming up with the wrong one, maybe suggested by the fact that she is at a party held in a church basement and celebrating a sacrament.

Part Five

Hips; The First Job; Papa Who Wakes Up Tired in the Dark; Born Bad; Elenita, Cards, Palm, Water

Summary

Esperanza, Nenny, Lucy, and Rachel are talking about getting "Hips." Esperanza gives the others some scientific information learned from Alicia and says one has to practice walking with hips; Nenny says that the walk is to rock a baby inside you to sleep. The girls are jumping rope, and their thoughts fit in with their jump-rope steps and rhymes. Everyone makes up an original rhyme for double-dutch, but Nenny uses a worn-out old rhyme.

In "The First Job," Esperanza gets a summer job in a photo-development establishment where her aunt works. She needs the money in order to go to the Catholic high school, and she lies about her age in order to get the job, which she finds easy but tiring. She is nervous in her new workplace; at last a man befriends her, but he does so only to take sexual advantage of her.

Early one morning, Esperanza's father tells her that her grandfather is dead. He weeps, and Esperanza thinks how she would feel should *he* die. As the eldest child, she must tell the others the news. She knows her father will go to Mexico for the funeral.

Esperanza has an aunt who has been ill for years, lying in bed while her husband and two sons take care of her, the house, and each other, a job they don't do too well. Esperanza has sometimes read to her from her library books and once read one of her own poems to her aunt. Aunt Lupe told her to keep writing. Now, in "Born Bad," Esperanza is ashamed because she and Lucy and Rachel have, for fun, imitated Aunt

Lupe's voice and mannerisms, laughing at the way she did and said things. Esperanza's mother happened to see them and was angry, and now Lupe has died.

Esperanza goes to visit a "witch woman" in "Elenita, Cards, Palm, Water." This person knows how to tell fortunes by various means and also knows how to make things happen by magic. Elenita sends her children out of the room while she tells Esperanza's fortune. Esperanza is disappointed because she wants in particular to find out if she will have a house. Finally she asks Elenita, who says Esperanza will have a home in the heart—something Esperanza doesn't understand.

Commentary

Mango Street darkens in this section of chapters, which ends with Esperanza's questions concerning her life and future. In between, she experiences death, which affects her in complex ways. Her father's grief shakes her; suddenly she is in the position of comforting him as though he were the child and she the adult. At the same time, she is suddenly aware that he, too, will die. Her aunt's death causes her to feel great guilt, because she and her friends have mocked this sick woman's grotesque mannerisms.

Aunt Lupe, ill for a long time, has been a sort of fixture in Esperanza's life, her condition both frightening and repulsive to the girl. Now the person who praised her poetry is dead. And with her aunt's death, Esperanza moves closer toward her own mortality: Why was this woman, young and pretty once, struck down? Finally Esperanza can only believe that death does not choose for a reason but merely points at random to its next victim. It is an unsettling and very adult thought. The combined emotions surrounding these deaths bring dreams to Esperanza and her friends, and they discover for the first time that the dead can haunt the living.

Part of the horror Aunt Lupe's illness has inspired in Esperanza and her friends (who have visited Lupe together) may stem from the condition of the sick woman's house and the kind of care she has received from her husband and sons. Traditionally, the wife and mother is in charge of *all* housework, including cooking and cleaning but also, often, repairs, painting, and refinishing as well. Lupe has obviously not been able to hold up her end of this household work, and (as Esperanza makes clear in this chapter) her husband and sons resent having to perform these "feminine" chores and show their resentment by performing them badly or not at all. The dishes pile up in the sink, Lupe's sheets are dirty, as are the walls and ceiling. Like the other adult women Esperanza knows and will come to know, her aunt serves as a sort of model; this is one possible future for Esperanza herself, and a terrible, terrifying one. If men are always possessed of the power in sexual and marital relationships, the men in Lupe's life are using that power cruelly against their wife and mother, and clearly no one expects any other kind of behavior from them.

Darkness enters these chapters in another way as well. While some of the changes associated with growing older are exciting (the blossoming of the womanly figures that the girls will need to know how to deal with) and others at least somewhat positive (Esperanza's feeling that science is "on her side" and her imaginative self-assurance, despite the fact that these developments are carrying her "light years" beyond and away from Nenny), still other changes are disturbing.

Literary Device

The further Esperanza gets from childhood, the less she can be protected—and, ironically, the more she is in need of protection. Her parents are determined that she continue to go to Catholic schools, where they believe (perhaps with justification) that she will be *morally* safer than in a public high school. This eventuality may still be some time in the future, but in order to make it possible, Esperanza now needs to get a job and thus needs to look older than she is. This is a family decision, but once away from her family and neighborhood, Esperanza is in territory that holds dangers for a young girl who has managed to appear older than her age. In another foreshadowing of what will happen to her in a later chapter, Esperanza in her innocence is taken advantage of by a man who pretends to be her friend. Forced by circumstances to enter this part of the adult world on her own, she is initiated into its sexual dangers in a distressing and—to a young girl—frightening way.

Style & Language

A note is in order, at this point, on the book's structure. As a coming-of-age novel, *Mango Street* takes its plot from the tensions that exist for its protagonist—between childhood and adulthood, between identification with family and community and the discovery of self-identity and independence, and between the unconventional life of the mind and the conventional "feminine" choices of marriage and family. Aware of these tensions but not able or willing to verbalize them, still Esperanza is concerned about what choices she can and ought to make.

But telling her own story, she can relate only some things that happen, some things she does, that seem to her important. She cannot tell us the plot, nor even select and order the incidents she does tell us, at least not in such a way that would show she is somehow aware of their relationship and meaning. That selection and ordering is up to the clever writer, Sandra Cisneros, and its interpretation as plot is up to us—the clever readers.

The book's structure, as we have noted, seems to be more or less linear; that is, the incidents and Esperanza's reflections seem to be taking place in more or less chronological order, or at least there is no reason to believe they are *not* told at least more or less in the order of their happening. But while some chapters seem to follow in direct succession, there seem to be relatively long periods of time between other chapters. At this point, it seems safe to say that Esperanza's family moved into the house on Mango Street during the summer before Esperanza entered the seventh grade. The first 14 chapters take place during that summer, while Esperanza is still getting acquainted with the neighborhood. Beginning with "Darius and the Clouds," Esperanza is in school, but it seems that "Hips" may be the last chapter whose incidents take place during the school year. Will Esperanza enter the eighth grade in the next fall? She will say specifically, near the end of the book, that Sally (a classmate) is not yet in the eighth grade. And she will say, also, in one of the final chapters, that she has lived in the house on Mango Street for just one year.

Whatever the exact timetable of these incidents, the chapters from "The First Job" through the end of the book seem to recount the events of only one summer—the last summer of childhood for Esperanza, and, as such, one of those long, long seasons that seem in retrospect to have gone on forever. Although it has its idyllic moments, it is not a happy summer for Esperanza. Still keeping her own counsel for the most part, she is not given to rehearsing her worries, but we know that she has them when she tells us she has gone to a "witch-woman," a fortune-teller, to learn her future. What Elenita tells her is a conventional, canned sort of fortune. Esperanza wants to believe—at the same time that she wants *not to know* (she must force herself not to run into the other room to watch Bugs Bunny)—but at last, she must tell the fortune-teller what she wants to hear.

Glossary

Tahiti   one of the Society Islands, in the South Pacific; perhaps Lucy (or whoever says this) is thinking about the Polynesian dances performed by Tahitians.

merengue   a fast dance that originated in the Dominican Republic.

tembleque   (Spanish) a trembling fit; "the shakes"—i.e., delirium tremens.

"Engine, engine number nine. . . ."   a very old jump-rope rhyme.

abuelito   (Spanish) a familiar diminutive of *abuelo* (grandfather).

está muerto   (Spanish) he is dead.

Joan Crawford   an American movie actress, most popular in the 1930s, 1940s, and 1950s.

"the sickness. . . ."   Aunt Lupe's illness; apparently Esperanza is somewhat confused about whether her aunt was ill or injured in some sort of accident; what she says about her having been swimming, and the fact that she was paralyzed, suggests that Lupe contracted polio, relatively common in the 1950s and often spread through the use of swimming pools.

The Waterbabies   (really, *The Water-Babies*) a popular novel written for children, first published in 1863, by English novelist Charles Kingsley (1819–75).

los espíritus   (Spanish) the spirits.

Part Six

Geraldo No Last Name; Edna's Ruthie; The Earl of Tennessee; Sire; Four Skinny Trees

Summary

Marin goes to dances whenever she can. One night, she danced with Geraldo, a young man from Mexico who didn't speak English. Later Geraldo was struck by a car, and Marin went with him to the hospital and waited while he died. He had no identification.

"Edna's Ruthie" is the daughter of a woman who owns the apartment house next door. She is odd (the only adult, Esperanza says, who likes to play), dresses strangely, and can't make decisions. She is living with her mother, although she is supposedly married and has a home of her own. Esperanza shows Ruthie her library books and once recited a poem for her.

"The Earl of Tennessee" is a man who lives in Edna's basement apartment, near where Esperanza and her friends gather. Sometimes he tells them to be quiet, because he sleeps days and works nights. He speaks with a southern accent, has two little dogs, and is said to have a wife who occasionally comes to visit him in his musty basement; several people have seen her, but they cannot even come close to agreeing on what she looks like.

A boy called "Sire" stares at Esperanza whenever she passes his house, but she refuses to act scared. Once she stared back. Sire fascinates Esperanza; her parents tell her to leave him alone. He has a girlfriend called Lois, and their relationship also fascinates Esperanza. She leans out her bedroom window at night and tries to imagine what it would be like if Sire held her and kissed her.

In "Four Skinny Trees," Esperanza describes the four trees that grow in front of her house. Esperanza identifies with the trees and says they too don't belong where they are, but that they use their anger to survive. She learns from them, she says, to keep going.

Commentary

Theme

The chapters in this group might be said to have a common theme—mystery, or perhaps ambiguity. The first four are concerned with people, incidents, and feelings that are mysterious to Esperanza in various ways. The fifth epitomizes the emotional ambiguity of adolescence, the feelings of anger and longing that Esperanza usually keeps within herself.

Geraldo "No Last Name" is himself a mystery that will never be solved, because he is dead and no one knows anything about him except that he was from Mexico. His family will wonder what became of him—probably they were depending upon money he was sending home—but there will be no way for them to find out. Marin, although she had danced with him, knew nothing about him and couldn't remember where he said he worked. And why was Marin with him at that hour? Had he seemed likely to take her to a fine house far away? Whatever the case, he had touched her deeply enough that she waited at the hospital, where he was not saved—although he might have been, had he been luckier in several regards (including, Esperanza implies, luckier in his color, language, profession, and economic status—but then he might not have been walking at 3 a.m. with Marin).

In fact, there is probably only one place where a young man who rents a sleeping room in the city might have been going with Marin at 3 a.m. Whether they were going to his room or leaving it, walking to where Marin might catch a train or bus home, we will never know, as Marin is not heard from again in the book. But we know that Marin, surely no older than 15 and probably not quite that, would not go to a young man's room without being "in love" with him, even if that love was of only a few hours duration, even if she had never learned his last name. Of course she would not be cold enough to leave him dying alone, although her presence in the waiting room could not help him.

Style & Language

In the last few paragraphs of "Geraldo," Esperanza's voice seems to change slightly, to become older, less puzzled about who Geraldo was and what Marin was doing with him. As elsewhere in the book—for example, in the last paragraph of "Marin"—Cisneros here seems to shift almost imperceptibly from Esperanza's 12-year-old voice into the voice of the woman whom Esperanza will become. Perhaps, of course, these are merely instances of Esperanza's jumping forward to age 25 or so, as she sometimes seems to jump backward to 9 or 10; such time-travel is rather common in early adolescence.

What Esperanza does not understand about Edna's daughter Ruthie is why, if Ruthie has a house and a husband of her own, she would choose to stay on Mango Street. In fact, as Esperanza's description of Ruthie and her behavior makes clear, this grown-up woman who likes to play is what adults might call "crazy"; unable to deal with whatever demands her adult life made of her, she has come back to the country of childhood where she is more comfortable. Ruthie, like Geraldo, is someone who might arguably have found help in the "system" had she lived in a middle-class neighborhood (and certainly had she lived in an upper-class one), and/or had her family and friends thought of her problems as the kind that professionals ought to deal with. But, as typical in working-class neighborhoods—at least in earlier years, and probably as late as the 1960s—the "crazy" person, whether seriously delusional or merely eccentric, is seen neither as someone who needs to be "cured" nor as someone who ought to be hidden away, kept out of "normal" society. Ruthie will fare better than Geraldo, of course; her condition is not going to kill her, at least not immediately, and she is almost certainly happier than, say, a wealthy industrialist's daughter with similar deficiencies, who would probably be institutionalized. But her teeth are rotting, her eyesight is bad, her mental condition may deteriorate and her mother will surely grow old and die, leaving Ruthie to become a neighborhood "character," uncared for by a future generation of children, unable finally to care for herself.

In Ruthie—as in similar women and men she encounters in the streets of her city—Esperanza sees yet another possibility for her own future. What would bring a cheerful, apparently once-capable woman to such a pass? Why, if she had a husband who *loved* her, would he not still love her and care for her? Ruthie tells Esperanza that she used to be a writer, and if this is true Esperanza has a reason to feel a degree of closeness between herself and Edna's daughter. Ruthie's creativity has not saved her. Esperanza memorizes a longish poem to recite for Ruthie—a fantastic, "crazy" poem by a man who wrote children's books and who played with children, preferring them apparently to adults.

The "Earl of Tennessee" is another adult neighborhood character, almost as sad in his own way as Ruthie in hers (and Esperanza, who sees Rosa Vargas' sadness clearly because Rosa herself sees it so well and with such vehemence, is only beginning to recognize sadness in these other adults). Earl is a lonely man, living alone in a damp basement, where he listens to country-and-western records that have been discarded from the jukeboxes he repairs for a living. He works nights—a standard shift for men in his trade, who get calls from bars where the patrons complain loudly and bitterly if their jukebox is out of order—and takes his two little dogs with him for company. He is kind to the neighborhood kids, giving them records and only occasionally coming out in the daylight and telling them to pipe down. And, on occasion, he brings a woman home during his off-duty hours, hurrying her into his apartment and not staying long. Esperanza, assuming the woman is his wife, is puzzled that no one who sees them together can agree on what the woman looks like. It has not yet occurred to her that each of them has seen a different woman.

Sire is an older neighborhood boy whom Esperanza is attracted to. She has been afraid of him, as young girls often are of the boys who stare at them; this is not fear of what he might *do* to hurt her, but rather the intimidation one feels when one is looked at in the way that Sire looks at her. "Sire" is probably a nickname—perhaps taken from a movie, for the word is an archaic form of address for a man of authority. It is also a word that means *father*. Characteristically, Esperanza refuses to be intimidated; still, Sire bothers her, and the fact that her parents don't like him probably has an effect opposite to their intent. On the other hand, she doesn't seem to be jealous that Sire has a girlfriend, a dainty girl who lets Sire tie her shoes. Esperanza fantasizes what it would be like to *be* that girl, what it would be like if Sire were to kiss her. Since Esperanza's first kiss from a man was forced upon her and must have been unpleasant in the extreme, her interest in Sire is a hopeful sign that she has recovered—or will soon recover—from that insult to her young womanhood.

Literary Device

A recurring image in *The House on Mango Street* is that of a woman at a window, leaning on her elbow, watching the world outside her house or room. We see it first in "My Name," where Esperanza says she doesn't want to "inherit" this position from the great-grandmother whose namesake she is. It is the image of a captive, someone inside looking out, someone taking the world in through her eyes. Later Esperanza will associate this image with "Rapunzel," the fairy-tale princess whose lover reached the tower where she was imprisoned by climbing up Rapunzel's long hair. The women in *Mango Street* who assume this position are sometimes married, but they all seem to be, like Rapunzel (and like Marin, who stands in her family's doorway), waiting for someone to come and change their lives. Now, in "Sire," Esperanza herself leans out her window, wishing she were older and could stay out at night. She wants to be rescued from her tower, taken away from the parents who think boys like Sire are "punks" and girls like Lois, his girlfriend, sluts. Traditionally, that kind of rescue is by a young man; this is the way Esperanza's thoughts are now turning.

Character Insight

And, in "Four Skinny Trees," still leaning out her window, Esperanza is overtaken by a wave of adolescent angst, which she survives by almost literally seizing the branches of the four trees growing from the sidewalk in front of her house. As a poet, Esperanza may feel more than others a need to associate with natural beings; she has spoken of this need in "Darius and the Clouds," and it is true that in many cultures trees are special creatures, full of spiritual meaning for human beings. This too seems to be a sign of Esperanza's emotional health, for she is able to project her feelings of alienation, anger, intensity, and need for secrecy onto the trees, while taking *from* them their strength, determination, and deep-rootedness.

Glossary

"Pretty, too, . . ."   i.e., good to look at; in Latino dialects, "pretty" is an acceptable adjective to be applied to a young man.

"cumbias, salsas, . . . rancheras. . . ."   Latin dances fashionable in the middle 1960s.

kitchenettes   i.e., "efficiency" apartments; small apartments consisting basically, apart from a bathroom, of a single room with a kitchenette.

babushka   a headscarf folded into a triangle and tied under the chin.

Marlon Brando   an American movie actor, first popular in the 1950s.

"The Walrus and the Carpenter"   a "nonsense" poem from *Through the Looking-Glass* (a sequel to *Alice's Adventures in Wonderland*) by Lewis Carroll (1832–98).

45 records   seven-inch recorded vinyl disks to be played on a phonograph at 45 rpm (rotations per minute); each usually has a three-to-four minute song recorded on each side.

Part Seven

No Speak English; Rafaela Who Drinks Coconut & Papaya Juice on Tuesdays; Sally; Minerva Writes Poems; Bums in the Attic

Summary

Mamacita is what Esperanza and her friends call the wife of a neighbor in "No Speak English." This man saved to bring his wife to the U.S., and one day she arrived with her baby boy and lots of luggage. Since then she hasn't come out of their apartment; some say it's because she's too fat or because she's afraid of the stairs, but Esperanza believes it's because she can't speak English. The woman is homesick and cries for the house where she used to live, but her husband says they *are* home. He tells her to speak English, but she won't or can't; now her baby is learning to talk, and he talks English.

In "Rafaela Who Drinks Coconut & Papaya Juice on Tuesdays," Esperanza tells of a young woman whose husband goes out every Tuesday night with his friends and locks her in the apartment. She leans out the window watching the children in the street, listening to the music from the bar where she wishes she could go to dance. Rafaela lowers a dollar from her window on a string and asks the girls to go get her a fruit juice drink.

"Sally" is a girl Esperanza knows. At school Sally dresses seductively; before she goes home, she changes her style so that her strict father will not notice how she has looked. Sally and her best friend had a bitter fight, and now she has no friend. Boys laugh and tell stories about Sally that Esperanza says are not true.

Another girl, Minerva, not much older than Esperanza, has two babies and a husband who keeps leaving but coming back. In "Minerva Writes Poems," Esperanza says that she and Minerva talk and show their poems to each other. Minerva is always sad, always in some kind of trouble. One day she tells her husband to get out and stay out, but he comes back, she lets him in, and then he beats her up again. Minerva asks Esperanza what she can do.

In "Bums in the Attic," Esperanza describes the house she wants to have someday. Her father is a gardener in a wealthy district, and on his day off he used to take his family to look at those places where he works. Now Esperanza refuses to go with them. Still, she wants a house like one of those; she says she'll let passing bums stay at her house, and they can sleep in the attic.

Commentary

The previous group of chapters found Esperanza being pulled by her emotions and physical feelings toward a sexual relationship with a young man. For Esperanza, such a relationship is still indefinite: "a boy" is what she dreams of; the only specific boy in her thoughts is one who now has a girlfriend, and Esperanza's interest in him seems more theoretical than practical. Yet the forces drawing her toward such a relationship with *someone* are powerful, coming from within herself and reinforced by her culture, which designates early marriage as the norm for young women. Now, in the chapters from "No Speak English" through "Minerva Writes Poems," Esperanza is concerned with women whose response to this imperative has resulted in terrible unhappiness. Thus the tension between what she feels and what she sees, what she *knows* of herself on two different levels, is again expressed.

Of the women described here, only Sally—who is certainly no older than Esperanza—is unmarried. She is, in the parlance of the time, a "bad girl," sexually promiscuous (if the boys' stories are true). Sally, at a fragile age when controlling the forces within and around her is well nigh impossible, is in a double bind. As she develops into a young woman, her father attempts to resist this inevitability by forcing her to hide her own sexuality (and, as we shall see in a later chapter, by beating Sally). Although her father is probably acting mainly out of a desire to protect her, his attitude and actions make Sally even more desperate to get away from him, and the only way she knows of doing this is to try to attract boys and young men, the very kind of behavior that gives rise to her father's fears and jealousies.

To make matters worse, Sally's behavior is socially counterproductive: promiscuity (or even its appearance) makes it more likely that boys will talk about her and try to get sexual favors from her but *less* likely that any one of them will court her, protect her from the others, and eventually rescue her from her father. Moreover, her behavior prevents the friendships with girls that might offer some relief from her unhappy situation. Only Esperanza is loyal to her—and Esperanza's loyalty will eventually be betrayed, for one facet of the sexual imperative that both girls feel (and to which Sally can find no alternative) is the feeling that other females are expendable. Whether this tendency is "natural" or culturally conditioned, U.S. culture in the 1950s and 1960s certainly reinforced it, approving solidarity among young men but promoting divisiveness and suspicion among young women.

The world of womanhood, into which Sally has already taken a wrong turn, is further represented here by three married women, at least one of whom is barely older than Esperanza herself. All three of these women have achieved what Sally wants, escape from the control of their fathers, and all three have reason to regret it. The happiest of the three, one might say, is the woman Esperanza and her friends call *Mamacita* ("little mama"). She has a husband who provides for her, a home, and a baby—in other words, she has reached the "goal" set for her by her culture. But she is entirely alienated and is becoming more so, as her child begins to speak a language she herself doesn't want to know. Significantly, Esperanza does not even know her name; this woman is entirely identified as a wife and mother, not as an individual.

The other two women in these chapters, Minerva and Rafaela, are prisoners in one way and another. Rafaela literally gets locked into her apartment while her husband goes out to play with his friends. This behavior on his part is not considered monstrous or insane in his culture (which, in this respect at least, is only an exaggeration of American culture in general in the middle 1960s); the husband has a right to lock up his wife, "protecting" her from men who might be attracted to what attracted *him*. Rafaela is one of her husband's possessions, useful when he has a use for her and kept in a safe place when he does not. All that marriage has done for Rafaela is to transfer her from one owner to another.

Minerva is less lucky, with a husband who beats her and then begs for forgiveness so that he can beat her again. Whether he is really sorry or not (and he may well be, for young men's socialization was and remains as potentially flawed as that of young women), Minerva knows of no way to get out of the cycle of abuse and apology. This is her husband, so she must do what he tells her—which means opening the door when he wants in.

Character Insight

Esperanza's response is in the form of a comfortable fantasy. She will have a big house of her own some day, and she will allow "bums"— meaning homeless people—to stay in her attic, because she knows what it is to be homeless. What Esperanza seems to mean is this: She is being driven by the changes she is experiencing and by her culture to make a choice she does not want to make. Esperanza loves her parents, and they seem to be much better parents than, for example, Sally's father and mother; this is not the point. She is disappointed in her family's small, ugly house, with its lack of privacy, where she must share a bedroom with the younger sister she loves but does not particularly like; this is not the point, either. Esperanza feels herself to be *homeless* in that there is no *place* for her in anything she knows, no precedent that she is aware of for a woman who wants to live a life of her own, not directed by her father *or* by a husband, and not—at the same time— required to renounce her existence as a sexual being in order to avoid being the property of a man.

Theme

Esperanza is a creative person, and the space she needs for herself is a space she must create—a roomy place, where she can be generous but can relegate others to "the attic" as guests but not necessarily friends. In Esperanza's fantasy, this is a real place, a large house different from the houses her friends dream of having in that it is hers alone, not contingent upon her becoming somebody's wife. But—as the playfulness of "Bums in the Attic" shows—Esperanza is beginning to realize that her dream house is also a metaphor, a symbol that stands for *partial* independence from other people. It may someday take on concrete reality, but until then it will be (and even after that it will remain) what Elenita foresaw for her: a home in the heart.

Glossary

"Mamasota"   "Big mama," emphasizing the woman's obesity.

fuchsia   a purplish-red color.

"¿Cuándo?"   (Spanish) "When?"

"¡Ay, caray!"   (Spanish) an expression of exasperation, something like "Damn it!" or "Oh, for heaven's sake!"

Rapunzel a princess in a fairy tale of European origin, imprisoned by a witch; her hair is very long, and the prince who comes to call on her climbs up to her tower by means of her hair.

Part Eight

Beautiful & Cruel; A Smart Cookie; What Sally Said; The Monkey Garden; Red Clowns

Summary

Esperanza feels she is ugly and that no man will ever want her, so she has decided not to wait. She admires the "Beautiful and Cruel" women in the movies, the ones who have their own power. She is practicing acting as if she had her own power, like a man.

Esperanza's mother tells her she was "A Smart Cookie" when she was young, but she let her life get away from her and now is unable to do things she would like to do. She tells Esperanza she quit school because she didn't have nice clothes, and she urges her daughter to go to school and study.

In "What Sally Said," Esperanza tells about her friend Sally, whose father beats her. Her father's sisters ran away and shamed their family; he fears that Sally will do the same. Sally gets permission to stay with Esperanza, but her father comes after her, begging her to come home. She does, and he beats her again.

There is a walled, abandoned garden in Esperanza's neighborhood where Esperanza and her friends go to play. The mysterious magic of the place draws them. One day Esperanza wants to run and roughhouse with other kids, but Sally would rather talk to some boys. The boys engage in some fairly innocent sex play with Sally; Esperanza is angry and tells the mother of one of them, who is unconcerned. Back in the garden, Sally tells Esperanza to go away.

Esperanza goes to a carnival with Sally, who leaves with a boy and tells Esperanza to wait by the "Red Clowns" near the tilt-a-whirl. Esperanza does so and is sexually assaulted.

Commentary

At this point, as *The House on Mango Street* approaches and then reaches the turning point from which its resolution will emerge, the book's tensions are drawn more clearly than ever. First, Esperanza makes a decision for herself that is a compromise between her emerging sexuality and her sense of the dangers sexuality holds for her. Then, in her mother's story, she clearly hears the terms of her conflict, the choice she must make. But her loyalty to Sally is met by careless betrayal, leading to disaster.

The decision Esperanza makes in "Beautiful and Cruel" is part real choice, part fantasy, and part compromise. Ultimately, she decides not to follow the accepted, culturally sanctioned example of such women as Rafaela, Minerva, *Mamacita*, Rosa Vargas—even Sally, Marin, and her own sister Nenny, who are waiting for someone to take them away from their childish dependency into what seems to be only an adult dependency. To Esperanza, if this is what "acting like a woman" amounts to, then she will begin to practice "acting like a man," which means in part that she will start letting somebody else carry out her dinner plate for her (for such things are really the only way she *can* "act like a man" while she is living in her parents' house). But the way Esperanza reaches this decision is interesting: She tells herself she is "ugly" and will not be courted. In part, she may believe this because she fails to meet her culture's standards of "beauty"—she is "skinny" (by which she probably means her breasts and hips are not yet fully developed). However, her "ugliness" seems to consist of failures in grooming, which suggests that Esperanza is using a familiar and helpful ploy to avoid going the way of Sally, Minerva, and the others—she is pretending to be unattractive; thus, she does not have to deal with the consequences of being "pretty."

Interestingly, too, she has *chosen* to be "beautiful and cruel"—that is, she has found a way to reject conventional femininity without rejecting *her* femininity. She fantasizes that she will adopt a sort of *femme fatale* image and behavior, attracting men but rejecting them, keeping her power for herself. Thus Esperanza's image of herself as "ugly" is in direct conflict with her image of herself as "beautiful and cruel"; one imagines that both are fantasies, comfortable as they alternate and cancel each other out.

Esperanza's mother's story, it seems, is less a cautionary tale than those of Rosa Vargas, Minerva, and *Mamacita*, but only because she is relatively happy in her marriage and her life, which in turn seems to be true partly because she is an intelligent and humorous woman. Here, she is smart enough not merely to tell Esperanza what to do (which would probably not accomplish anything), but instead to tell her what *she* has lost by quitting school. She *could have been* a serious singer or painter, but now must treat these talents as hobbies, embroidering flowers (a traditionally "feminine" art unlike painting) and singing in the kitchen. Without suggesting that she's sorry she had a family, she manages to convey the feeling that she wasted her talents and is not happy about having done so. This is a kind of reasoning Esperanza can understand and apply to her own life.

Interestingly, Esperanza's mother brings in a fictional character to reinforce her argument. "Madame Butterfly," the protagonist of the opera she has been singing, is a Japanese woman who falls in love with a Western naval officer, bears his child, waits passively for him to return as he has promised, and is eventually betrayed by him. Don't wait for a man to make a life for you, Esperanza's mother seems to be saying. Make your own life. She must recognize that Esperanza will probably be unhappy if she chooses the traditional path. It must worry her, too, to see that Esperanza has chosen to befriend Sally, a girl who seems headed in absolutely the wrong direction for Esperanza, for she knows the temptation is great to try to emulate Sally's looks, style, and apparent popularity with boys. Yet both of Esperanza's parents must recognize their daughter's generous spirit, for if anyone ever needed a friend, Sally does now.

But despite the efforts of Esperanza (and her parents) to shelter Sally, the other girl is seemingly doomed to live out the tragedy of her own unhappy family relationship. Clearly, Sally's father is stupidly and weakly repeating his own father's mistake, driving his daughter to the very sort of behavior that enrages him. Clearly Sally herself is not strong enough to leave home *except* (as we shall see) with another man, although Esperanza's parents have invited her to live with the Cordero family. By now, in fact, Sally has probably begun to define herself as someone whose function is to inspire passion—sexual passion or rage—in men. And so, probably without understanding what she is doing, Sally uses Esperanza as a companion and enjoys her friend's loyalty and admiration without taking the trouble to return the friendship. Sally's carelessness results in disaster in "Red Clowns"; however, Esperanza has a forewarning of it in "The Monkey Garden," if she only knew how to read her friend's signals.

Literary Device

The "monkey garden" is one of *Mango Street*'s strongest symbolic images, like the four trees in front of Esperanza's house, the house itself, the woman leaning out a window on her elbow. Both beautiful and frightening, both an Eden and a wasteland, this place attracts Esperanza both for its strong and mysterious sexual overtones (in the rank, lux-uriant growth and the memory of the monkey) and for the fact that it seems a wilderness within her urban neighborhood, the sort of natu-ral place she craves. Here she can discard the civilized shell of the adult she is becoming for one last fling at being a child. When Sally seems to be threatened by Tito and the other boys, Esperanza is angered both for the threat to her friend—which is a real threat at least in essence, although Sally seems to invite it—and for the doom it spells to her own childish self; these sexual games mark the end of childhood.

Character Insight

The misery Esperanza feels later, when she wishes to die, is real as well, but it is not entirely embarrassment and anger. In part she is feel-ing but trying not to acknowledge Sally's betrayal. (Is Sally the "best friend" for whom Esperanza has longed? Almost certainly, Sally has con-fided sexual secrets—real or fantasized, probably a little of both—to her, which suggests Esperanza has entrusted her own secrets to Sally.) In part, Esperanza is miserable for her own loss of innocence, which has not yet occurred except symbolically, as she is thrust out of the garden.

And then her loss occurs in fact, when Sally disappears with a boy, leaving Esperanza alone to be preyed upon by other boys or men. The details of what actually happens to her at the carnival are not clear; how-ever, given her clear and unemotional description (in "The First Job") of a relatively minor assault, we can be sure that this one is far more serious. Esperanza's language in "Red Clowns"—she addresses Sally, not the reader—is shocked, badly hurt, out of control in its syntax but nonetheless tremendously revealing in its tone and imagery. She says she does not remember what happened, but her reluctance to "tell it all" suggests that she does remember. And it seems that her friend's betrayal is as painful to her as the rape that resulted from it.

Glossary

Madame Butterfly   a character in the opera *Madama Butterfly*, by Italian composer Giacomo Puccini (1858–1924).

comadres   (Spanish) women friends, girlfriends (to another woman).

Rip Van Winkle   a character in a tale ("The Legend of Sleepy Hol-low") by American writer Washington Irving (1783–1859).

Part Nine

Linoleum Roses; The Three Sisters; Alicia & I Talking on Edna's Steps; A House of My Own; Mango Street Says Goodbye Sometimes

Summary

Sally has married a young man in order to get away from her father. Now, Esperanza says in "Linoleum Roses," Sally has a house and furniture, but her husband gets violently angry some days, and he doesn't want her to see her friends, so they must go to see her while he is working. Most of the time, Sally stays in her new home and looks at the things that she and her husband own.

In "The Three Sisters," Lucy and Rachel's baby sister has died, and the family is having a traditional viewing and reception at home. Esperanza is nervous, but three old ladies are there and they reassure her. The three sisters look her over, tell her she is special, and tell her to make a wish. She does so, silently, and they say it will come true; then, as if they can read her mind, they tell her not to forget to come back to Mango Street.

Esperanza and Alicia are sitting on Edna's steps, talking. Esperanza says she wishes she were from somewhere other than Mango Street and the red house; Alicia tells her that she *is*, however, from Mango Street and that she will carry it with her and someday come back to it. In "A House of My Own," Esperanza tells us that someday she will live alone in a clean, quiet house with everything just as she wants it. And in the last chapter, Esperanza says that she likes to tell stories, that she belongs and does not belong in the house on Mango Street, and that sometimes writing the stories helps. She will go away someday, she says, but will come back for those who could not leave.

Commentary

The final five chapters of *Mango Street* offer a marriage, a death, three witches and a wish, a friendship, and a satisfying yet subtle resolution for Esperanza. We hear no more of the attack made upon her. Has she told anyone of it: her mother, for example? Perhaps not, for throughout the book—except in "The Red Clowns"—she has been somewhat secretive, something of a stoic, keeping her feelings and conflicts within herself, letting even the reader see only hints. She may have told Alicia, for Alicia seems now to be her confidante. Almost certainly she will not have told Sally, for to Esperanza that experience, which she did not want to talk about or remember in the first place, is something to be confided—if at all—only to a truly *best* friend, and it is now clear to Esperanza that Sally is not her real friend.

Still Sally is a "friend," in the same sense that Cathy (Queen of Cats) was a friend very early in the book. Part of Esperanza's stoicism is that she seems to accept people for what they are, knowing they will not change in radical ways; as she has said several times of her sister, "That's how she is." So Esperanza goes to visit Sally, now probably approaching her fourteenth birthday, in the home Sally shares with her new husband, where she is kept a virtual prisoner by this "marshmallow salesman" with a violent temper. Esperanza says she knew this would happen; now it has happened and there is nothing to be done about it. Esperanza tells this in a flat, unemotional tone. She knows Sally is not "in love" but was only governed by a need to escape her unbearable life.

Esperanza has now grown beyond her wish to emulate Sally. That wish may have extended only to matters of makeup and style, of course, but it seems linked (by her association of Sally with the queen Cleopatra) to Esperanza's decision to be "beautiful and cruel"—that is, to pursue relationships with boys in which she herself had the upper hand, the "power." Her experience at the carnival has taught her that she does not yet have that kind of power and has shown her graphically that what some people call "love" may be an exercise of physical power directed against her. Whatever she may do in the future, whether or not she continues to visit Sally, whether or not she enters into a mutual relationship with a boy, Esperanza for now seems in effect to have said good-bye to Sally and to have moved beyond that earlier phase of sexual curiosity and desire. That tension has been released, in a very negative way, and that part of Esperanza's inner conflict has been, for a time at least, resolved. Now she is faced with her original problem, the question of who she is, where she belongs, how to escape from Mango Street (and her childhood, and her family)—how, in brief, to become the adult that she wishes to be, the strong woman who controls her own life.

Style & Language

Traditionally, in folk tales the world over, young women are sometimes guided at the beginning of their journeys through life by older women, crones even, who offer practical advice and/or magic charms. Esperanza has already sought such advice—and perhaps charms as well—from the "witch woman" Elenita. Now, in the magical and powerful presence of the dead, she finds unexpected help in the persons of three elderly women, Lucy and Rachel's aunts (probably, given their ages, great-aunts). Esperanza does not tell their names; perhaps she does not know them. She describes them, however, in language that sets an atmosphere of real magic, ancient beliefs mixed with Christianity, and, although they offer her mundane gifts (chewing gum and Kleenex), they are obviously, in her mind and the reader's, real, powerful—and good—witches.

Alicia too is an older woman and the giver of a gift. What the old women have told Esperanza is repeated by Alicia, who is now (although Esperanza, always economical with language, does not say it in so many words) her real friend; their friendship is sealed by Alicia's gift and by a confidence, for Esperanza tells Alicia out loud what she wished for in silence in the room with the dead baby. And if her guidance by the three sisters suggests she will choose a form of magic, Alicia's influence suggests that she will also choose education. Thus Esperanza's resolution, at the end of *The House on Mango Street*, is revealed to be ambiguous, ironic, but real: She will escape Mango Street but will never escape it, for it is part of her. "You will always be Mango Street," Alicia tells her, using the same figure of speech that Lucy inadvertently uses early in the book: "Me, I'm Texas." Esperanza's escape from Mango Street (and from her childhood) must be by a magic of her own making, and it ironically involves her re-creation of the house, the neighborhood, and her childhood in stories. So she writes these stories sometimes, Esperanza says, and after she has written them, she is for a little while free of their power.

Glossary

"One night a dog cried . . . ." a traditional harbinger of death; a bird flying into a house, too, is supposed to foretell a death in the house.

CRITICAL COMMENTARIES: *"WOMAN HOLLERING CREEK" AND OTHER STORIES*

My Lucy Friend Who Smells Like Corn

My Lucy Friend Who Smells Like Corn; Eleven; Salvador Late or Early; Mexican Movies; Barbie-Q; 'Mericans; Tepeyac

Summary

Note: These 22 stories and sketches are grouped in three sections, each with one story that bears the same title as the section: "My Lucy Friend Who Smells Like Corn," "One Holy Night," and "There Was a Man, There Was a Woman." The stories will be considered here in groups for the most part, beginning with the first and second sections treated as two units.

The stories and sketches in this first section are set in childhood. Five are narrated by children; the two that are not ("Salvador Late or Early" and "Tepeyac") have children as main characters. "My Lucy Friend . . . ," whose speaker is a seven- or eight-year-old girl, is set in a poor neighborhood of a fairly large Texas city. The story has no plot; the speaker describes her friend, relates some of the things she and Lucy do together, and tells a few details about Lucy's house, family, and life. The speaker also reveals something about her own situation (she is living or staying with her grandmother). She likes Lucy and envies her having eight sisters; she feels that she and Lucy are like sisters.

"Eleven" takes place on the speaker's eleventh birthday. Rachel opens by saying other ages *before* eleven are still present inside the 11-year-old. She is in school; the teacher brings a sweater out of the coatroom and tries to determine its owner. A girl says it is Rachel's, and although Rachel denies it, the teacher puts the sweater on her desk and eventually makes her put it on, which brings her to tears. Later another girl remembers the sweater is *hers*, but Rachel is still upset and wishes she were invisible.

Salvador (in "Salvador Late or Early") is a small, apologetic boy who has no friends, comes from an very poor neighborhood, and (because his mother has a baby to care for) must get his two younger brothers ready for school, give them breakfast, and lead them by the hands to school and then home again.

In "Mexican Movies," the speaker is a young girl (six or seven years old) who describes a typical Saturday evening with her parents and little brother at a theater that shows Mexican movies. She tells about being sent to the lobby during sexy scenes and describes the furnishings of the theater and lobby and the things sold there; she tells about her favorite movies and talks about the things she and her brother do during the shows. Sometimes, she says, they go to sleep, and when the movie is over their parents carry them home to bed.

"Barbie-Q," set in Chicago in the early 1960s, features a nine- or ten-year-old speaker who talks to her friend directly about their Barbie dolls, their outfits, and the story they always enact with these dolls. One Sunday at a flea market, they find and buy Ken and several more Barbie outfits, friends, and relatives that have been damaged in a fire. These dolls smell smoky and have slight flaws, but the speaker and her friend don't care.

The speaker in "'Mericans" is Micaela, a young American girl visiting relatives in Mexico City. She and her brothers wait outside the church for their grandmother, who is inside praying. The older brother dozes in the sun; the younger one runs around shouting. They have been told not to leave, so they watch a procession of penitents approach the church. The speaker goes into the church for a while, then goes back outside. An American man and woman, tourists, take her brother's picture and are surprised he speaks English; he tells her they are "'Mericans."

The speaker in "Tepeyac" describes, in present tense, a typical weekday evening spent in Mexico City where she lives or is staying with her grandparents. She walks home with her grandfather from his shop, describing the places and people they pass. They count the steps from the street to their front door together and go in to their supper; from that house, she says, she will return to the U.S. Her grandfather will die, everything will change, and when she returns, years later, the house itself will seem different.

Commentary

Style & Language

One of the things Cisneros does best in her fiction is to evoke the *sensations*—sights, sounds, smells, tastes, palpable feelings—of being a child. The young speakers in this section (including the speaker in "Tepeyac," who "becomes" an adult only as her story ends) are excellently realized because they notice particulars and report them: the smashed-bug-on-the-windshield color inside a cat's-eye marble, the stickiness of a melting orange Popsicle, a child's shadow falling on a movie screen, every item on every table at a sidewalk flea market (or an inclusive selection). They report as well the intense emotions of childhood (from doing "loopity-loops" inside to wanting to disappear) and, all in all, capture perfectly for the reader the essence of being a child. We are reminded of Sandra Cisneros' early determination to write *out of* (although not necessarily *about*) her own particular experience and are able to see how that experience informs her characters' voices with authenticity.

Perhaps it is important, then, to remember that these stories can be read on different levels. Cisneros' characters will speak directly and honestly to young readers and will remind older readers of feelings we have—if we were lucky—known once but probably forgotten. Readers who share Cisneros' Latino background may recognize her perspective, but readers of other backgrounds will hardly be puzzled by it.

Of course, one way to read some of these stories (for example, "My Lucy Friend . . . ," "Mexican Movies," "Barbie-Q") is to see the children as "deprived": a poor, dirty little girl in 79-cent K-Mart flip-flops, sleeping in a fold-out chair in her grandparents' living room, whose best friend is one of nine children living in a shack; children whose mother, after sitting on her feet at the movies to avoid rats, must carry the little boy and girl up to their third-floor walk-up; an eight-year-old boy who shoulders the responsibility for two younger brothers; a pair of young Chicanas who must cut holes in an old sock to dress their blue-eyed Barbie dolls.

Character Insight

It is certainly true that the children of the working poor, in the U.S. as in many other countries, have traditionally been (and continue to be) deprived—nutritionally, medically, educationally, and in other ways as well—and that children belonging to racial and cultural minorities are not only statistically much more likely to be poor but are also frequently subjected to the insults of the bigoted majority. School- and university-aged readers, especially, need to be made aware of these truths if they are not already aware of them. But while such a reading of these stories is perhaps unavoidable, it would seem that to limit ourselves to such a reading would be to deprive ourselves not only of the stories' pleasures but of much of their "meaning" as well. These children do not feel themselves oppressed or deprived; they are experiencing the richness and sensuousness of childhood in environments where they are cared for and cared about. It is perhaps good to remember that they are not sitting sadly in front of television sets or playing endless video games, numbing themselves as their senses and imaginations slowly evaporate.

Theme

Thematically, the stories in this section introduce and develop the idea of displacement or alienation. This theme is only the faintest of whispers in "My Lucy Friend . . . ," where the speaker may be either living with her grandparents or staying with them temporarily (and where she calls Lucy a "Texas girl" as if she herself were *not* one), and is not present at all in "Mexican Movies," where the speaker seems absolutely happy and comfortable with her family. "Eleven," about the awful and sometimes irrational (from an adult point of view) misery of very early adolescence, finds its narrator, Rachel, wishing she were elsewhere—or nowhere—after her encounter with the dreaded sweater, which offends her in a way that must be almost purely subjective, for Phyllis Lopez has no qualms about claiming it later. Salvador, in "Salvador Late or Early" is forced—by circumstances, but also by his own good heart—to be older than his age, and we can see in this small, apologetic boy something of the humble, worried, perhaps sad man he will someday become.

In "Barbie-Q," the theme of alienation may be seen as an undercurrent beneath what the speaker actually *says*. One reading might see the flawed dolls as representing the girls' own self-image. As poor children, members of a cultural minority, the speaker and her friend (especially if we assume that they actually identify themselves with the dolls, perhaps not a wholly correct assumption) may see themselves as somehow "flawed," not as "the real thing," the future ideal American woman, white and middle-class (mean-eyed and "bubbleheaded"—that is, wearing the Jackie Kennedy bouffant), but instead as somehow a kind of cut-rate, smoke-damaged version whose defects can be hidden but will always be there. (To support this reading, we may note that in a later story, "Never Marry a Mexican," the adult narrator describes her ex-lover's wife unflatteringly as "a red-headed Barbie doll.") Another possible reading, of course, based quite firmly in the narrator's words, is one in which the girls, being fairly sophisticated, know that their dolls are just dolls and have, in their own regard, as healthy a sense of self-worth as possible for children who have been given the idea that an eye-lash brush is a necessary piece of equipment for a young woman.

Displacement is at the heart of "'Mericans," where the children—strangers in their father's country, their relatives' city, and their grand-mother's church—are further alienated from each other by gender, with the little boys calling each other "girl" as an insult. The narrator is beginning to be alienated from herself, wanting to cry but stopping because "crying is what *girls* do." Finally, in a nice bit of irony, two Americans with a camera appear, looking for a picturesque subject. Spotting the children, they do not recognize their fellow U.S. citizens but, instead, assume they are little Mexicans whom they can photograph for their travel album.

And, in the final story of the section, "Tepeyac," the theme of alienation appears in a number of ways. The narrator, as a child, is visiting here, meaning it is not *her* place (although she tries to make it hers by naming every person and landmark she passes, counting the very steps between her grandparents' gate and the front door). She is about to return to *her* country, but that is not hers either, for she calls it "that borrowed country"—as her grandfather no doubt sees it. When she comes back, years later, she will find that nothing is left but her memories, as unreal as the painted backdrops used by souvenir photographers in the square (as she remembers them). The only real thing, perhaps the spirit of the district as it existed/exists on the evening she remembers, will be unnamed and unnamable, and her grandfather will have taken it with him (she says) to his "stone bed."

Literary Device

The irony of this speaker's displacement would function no matter where the story were set, but it is especially sharp here, for Tepeyac is one of the holy centers of ancient *and* modern Mexican culture, a place sacred to the Mother-Goddess Tonantzin and also to the Virgin of Guadalupe, who appeared miraculously to the Indian peasant Juan Diego there. The narrator's grandfather, she says, is the only person who does not believe in this miracle. Later, as an adult returning to Tepeyac, the granddaughter of an alienated Mexican, she will be twice alienated, a member neither of her own culture nor of his. What she will have, however, will be her memories, precise and exact—or perhaps imprecise and inexact—as memories can be, after everything they are based upon has faded into the past.

Glossary

"También yo te quiero/ y te quiero feliz" (epigram to the section)
I also love you / and want you happy.

nixtamal a mixture of ground corn and lime for making tortillas.

Abuelita Grandma; affectionate diminutive of *abuela*, grandmother.
(Unless otherwise noted, non-English words here are Spanish.)

churros long donuts.

¡Qué saquen a ese niño! Get that kid out of here!

la ofrenda box offering box.

tlapaléria a little lunch stand.

cerro hill.

La Virgen de Guadalupe The Virgin of Guadalupe, i.e. St. Mary,
mother of Jesus, as she appeared miraculously to Juan Diego in
1531 on the hill of Tepeyac near this church.

sastreria seamstress; tailor.

¿Quieres chicle? Want some gum?

La Basílica de Nuestra Señora The Basilica of Our Lady.

tlapaleria a hardware store.

sopa de fideo noodle soup.

carne guisada meat stew.

One Holy Night

One Holy Night; My *Tocaya*

Summary

The speaker in "One Holy Night" is an eighth-grade girl living in Chicago with her grandmother and uncle, immigrants from Mexico. She tells the events of the story in past tense: She was selling fruits and vegetables from a pushcart on Saturdays, and she fell in love with one of her customers, known on the street as Boy Baby, who told her his name was Chaq Uxmal Paloquín and that he was descended from Mayan kings. He lived in a room above the garage where he worked, and in a few weeks, she went there with him. He showed her many weapons, and they made love. When she went home that night, she forgot to bring the pushcart and made up a story about its being stolen. She was not allowed to leave the house then, and by the time her grandmother learned the truth, Boy Baby had left. Then the narrator found that she was pregnant. They learned Boy Baby had a sister who was a nun in Mexico; the sister did not know his whereabouts but revealed that his real name was Chato (meaning "fat-face") and that he was from a poor peasant family with no Mayan blood. The narrator's grandmother sent her to cousins in Mexico to have her baby; while still waiting for its birth, she has learned that her beloved was recently arrested for the serial killing of women.

Another teen-aged girl, Patricia Chávez, is the narrator of "My *Tocaya*," set in San Antonio. This girl tells the story of another Patricia, slightly younger, who went missing at the age of 13. The family of the missing girl advertised for her to no avail; then a body found in a ditch was identified as hers. Soon after the funeral, however, Patricia Benavídez appeared and announced that she wasn't dead; her family had identified the wrong girl.

Commentary

Here the simplicity of the child's vision and emotion gives way to the complexity of adolescence in the relative complexity of these stories, in which the themes are love and sex, birth and death, truth and lies.

The two narrators, "Ixchel" (the Mayan name her lover gives her; she is never otherwise identified) and Patricia Chávez, present themselves in very different voices, the one serious and traditional, the other flip and hard-edged; they are responding in different ways to the knowledge of sexual love and betrayal, of women's vulnerability, and of death.

For "Ixchel," there are two realities, one sacred and one profane, and she has chosen the sacred one with its mythic truths. Her sexual initiation is her initiation into this sacred world and has nothing to do with pleasure or the social choices that concern, for example, Patricia Chávez. "Ixchel" seems to sense intuitively a connection between love and death, grief and joy. The reader may wonder, but she does not, why "Chaq" shows her knives and guns but does not kill her as he apparently has killed other young women. In the conventional, ordinary world, there is no resolution to her story—or rather, there is the same resolution as her mother found: "Ixchel" will raise her baby and go on with her life, with no one but her friends Rachel and Lourdes knowing her secret and probably understanding it as imperfectly as the reader does. In the world of the sacred, "Ixchel" will go on believing the truth of what "Chaq" told her and of what happened to her on that "holy night." In the ordinary, profane world, her story is ridiculous, she was amazingly lucky, and her lover is probably insane; in the sacred world, the world that she and "Chaq" believe in, which is outside *time*, everything is happening as fate dictates.

Patricia Chávez lives in a world in which nothing out of the ordinary has happened to her; the "death and resurrection" of her *tocaya* (the other Patricia), which she reports, is merely a stupid mistake, a nine-day wonder for the papers and television. The fact that the mistake was made at all suggests that Patricia Benavídez's parents are careless and that the girl will probably run away again, tired of working in her father's taco shop and tired of being beaten. Patricia Chávez is not really concerned.

But by the magic of naming, which Patricia C. acknowledges in calling Patricia B. her *tocaya*, or namesake, the two are doubles (like Poe's William Wilson and his nameless double). The dead girl, too, is another double (a triple?), for she has no name until Patricia B.'s parents "name" her by mistake. That means that, on a symbolic level, what happens to one happens to all three. In one sense, Patricia B. *has* died and returned to life, as has *her tocaya*, Patricia C.; in another sense, both of them are as bereft of life as the third girl, the one found in a ditch. The sacred and profane exist side by side in this story, too, but here the sacred world—the world of religion, of death and resurrection—is reduced to empty "theology" talks like "Heavy Metal and the Devil" that Patricia Chávez rightly derides, without knowing of anything *more* meaningful.

While "Ixchel," in the previous story, has an intuitive faith in the mythos of her parents' culture (the "truth" told her by "Chaq") to sustain her, Patricia B. (and by extension her *tocaya*, the narrator here) must resort to a phony British accent and the pseudo-sophistication of U.S. teen culture to escape the unhappiness of her family life—an escape that (by extension) the third girl failed of achieving. And while "Chaq's" lies to "Ixchel" represent (at least to him and her) something mythically *truer* than the facts, Patricia B.'s parents' lies to the media (ironically saying essentially the same thing "Chaq" says: "She was my little princess") are so shamelessly untrue that Patricia C. doesn't even bother to identify them as lies.

Glossary

"Me importas tú, y tú, y tú/ y nadie más que tú" (epigram to the section)   Only you matter to me, you, you / and no one else but you.

Tikal, Tulum, Chichén   Ancient cities of the Maya on the Yucatan Peninsula.

dar a luz   have a baby; give birth (literally, "give light," in the sense of bringing an infant into the light, giving birth).

Alegre   Cheerful, happy, lighthearted.

tocaya   a namesake, or another person who shares one's name.

Dolorosa and Soledad   street names; they translate as *sorrow* and *solitude*.

Y te quiero mucho   and I love you very much.

Virgencita, Cuídala   Blessed Virgin, Watch Over Her

There Was a Man, There Was a Woman—Part One

Woman Hollering Creek; The Marlboro Man; *La Fabuloso*: A Texas Operetta; Remember the Alamo

Summary

"Woman Hollering Creek" is told in third person. Its central character, a well-brought-up young Mexican woman named Cleófilas, bored with her life, tired of waiting on her father and brothers, and inspired by the romance of soap operas, has married a Texas man and moved north of the border; in due time she has borne a son. Her husband, whom she has discovered is stupid, boorish, and unfaithful, beats her, and she would leave him but she doesn't speak English and doesn't know how to get away. Pregnant again, she visits her doctor and confides in the office nurse, who calls a friend; the friend picks up Cleófilas and takes her and her little boy to the bus station to return to her father.

Two voices speak in "The Marlboro Man," a dialogue between women friends about "Durango," whom a friend of one of the women used to date and upon whom the other used to have a bad crush, although she never met him. The one who *had* met him shares some information about him, but since there have been several "Marlboro Men" in ads and billboards, the two decide they don't know if they're even talking about the same "Durango."

"*La Fabulosa*: A Texas Operetta" is narrated by a voice that might be one of the speakers in the previous story. She tells the story of Carmen Barriozábal, a legal secretary in San Antonio who had a brief affair with a young corporal in the army, then dismissed him and took up with a Texas senator. The corporal tried to kill her and himself, but failed; there are different versions, says the narrator, of what became of him, but Carmen broke up with her senator and started seeing a professional wrestler.

The speaker in "Remember the Alamo" is a man (Rudy Cantú, stage name Tristán) who, after suffering homosexual abuse as a child, has become a professional dancer. He describes his life, his relationship with his mother, sisters, and father, and the wild adulation of his fans—a tribute well deserved, he suggests. He says he has successfully forgotten the squalor and sadness of his earlier life; he has left all that behind for the artistry and the daring of his career. Tristán's narrative is occasionally interrupted by groups of names: all Latin names, masculine and feminine.

Commentary

The story "Woman Hollering Creek" turns on Cleófilas's question about the creek's name—why is the woman hollering, from anger or from pain? The name in Spanish, "La Gritona," means the same as the English phrase; it is echoed by the names of Cleófilas's neighbors, Dolores and Soledad (Sorrow and Loneliness) and—as it turns out—also by the names of her two benefactors, Felice and Graciela (Happiness and Grace). It also reminds Cleófilas of "La Llorona," the Weeping (or Wailing) Woman, a figure in Mexican folklore, who according to critic Ana Maria Carbonell, is associated with water, is a maternal figure related to pre-conquest mother goddesses, and is said in some versions of her legend to have drowned her children. Sitting with her child by the creek, Cleófilas seems likely to follow the example of this folkloric "La Gritona," for she is desperate and feels she has nowhere to turn. The surprise for her is that there is an alternative to anger and pain, which she discovers when Felice drives her and the child across the creek and hollers for the pure joy of it, laughing at the name.

Felice and Graciela could be the two women in "The Marlboro Man," which is a satirical sketch about pop culture and the cult of celebrity. And one of them might be the narrator of "*La Fabulosa*: A Texas Operetta," which transforms Georges Bizet's opera *Carmen* (but not radically) into, well, a Texas operetta, with Carmen as Carmen, José as Don José, and the senator Camilo Escamilla as the toreador Escamillo. The grand-opera ending of the original, with Carmen dead and the soldiers leading José away, however, is ironically flattened here with José supposedly going to Mexico to become—what else?—a bull-fighter. Perhaps Cisneros is suggesting that everyday life in Texas is sometimes operatic.

Character Insight

"Remember the Alamo" is an enigmatic character sketch. Its narrator mentions long-ago sexual abuse—not the abuser's identity—only obliquely, near the final paragraph, in connection with the ugly world he wipes out when he dances. His tone throughout is one of swaggering bravado, tempered perhaps by a touch of self-mockery. Several times he refers to himself as "Tristán," in third person, suggesting both conceit and self-alienation. He is not, as one reviewer believes, a drag queen—that is, he does not adopt a female stage persona. His Tristán persona, as the name suggests, is hyper-masculine, not with the crude machismo of the "low rider types" he claims not to fear but with an elegant, disdainful—and dangerous—edge. He is proud of his appeal to both men and women, and (like some drag queens) he wears his persona off-stage; his life is part of his act.

Like his performance on stage, his off-stage life seems to involve taking chances—dancing, as he puts it, with death. His name for his stage dance partner is "thin death," and she symbolizes death itself. He seems to find her disgusting and despicable but believes she—like everyone else—can't help being "crazy about him." He knows she wants him. Perhaps the ongoing list names others whom death has wanted enough to take.

Glossary

"Me estoy muriendo/ y tú, como si nada . . ." **(epigram to the section)** "I'm dying / and you don't even care el"; from "Puñalada Trapera" by Tomás Méndez Sosa, sung by Lola Beltrán.

¡zas! like *voila!* (an exclamation meaning "Behold! There it is!).

"Pues, allá de los indios, quién sabe" "Well, must be from the Indians, who knows."

"¿entiendes? Pues" "Do you understand, then?"

la consentida the favorite (in the sense of favorite child, somewhat spoiled).

mi'jita affectionate term, shortening of *mi hijita*—my daughter.

Híjole equivalent to "Wow" or "Geez!" in English.

"Qué vida" "What a life."

for no *fulanita* for some nobody.

flaca thin.

"¿Verdad que me quieres, mi cariñito, verdad que sí?" "You love me, right, my love, isn't that so?"

"Te quiero" "I love you"; "I desire you."

Mi pedacito de alma desnuda My little piece of naked soul.

Wáchale, muchacha Watch out, girl.

There Was a Man, There Was a Woman—Part Two

Never Marry a Mexican; Bread; Eyes of Zapata

Summary

The speaker's name, in the first of these stories, is Clemencia; her mother, a Chicana, told her never to marry a Mexican. She says she will never marry, period. She doesn't trust men because she's helped too many be unfaithful to their wives. She describes the difference between her parents' backgrounds, tells something of her own life (she is an artist) and her alienation from her mother after her father's death. Then she addresses her ex-lover, Drew, a married man with a son. Years ago, before the son (now apparently in his late teens) was conceived, she was a student of his father, who seduced her and convinced her that he loved her. But in the end, he went back to his wife; he and Clemencia, however, continued their affair until a number of years after the boy was born. Alternately, Clemencia addresses the son himself, whom she now has as a lover. She feels she is in control of both of them, and she is vengeful, hating Drew's wife. She describes things she has done to hurt the wife and, indirectly, the man himself; she seems to be using the son, whom she despises, for this purpose only.

In "Bread," a sketch of less than one page, the speaker describes driving with her lover in the city (perhaps San Antonio) where she grew up; they are eating fresh bread. He remarks that it is a "charming city," and she remembers a child's death there.

"Eyes of Zapata" is told by Inés, the wife of Emiliano Zapata (an historical Mexican revolutionary leader [1879–1919]; Inés is a fictional character, but she is based on a real woman). Zapata is sleeping. Beside him, Inés muses about him and their life together. He is now a famous leader and has changed, she says, into a man who trusts no one. Their story emerges in a very non-linear fashion: In their youth, she went with him against her father's wishes and in due time bore two children. She and Zapata were never officially married, and he has other women, other children. Inés' life has always been difficult, especially during the revolutionary war; she has had to work hard just to feed her children, and Zapata has always put his work for the country ahead of his family. Inés has lived in poverty. Her mother was thought to be a witch and was killed; now the same stories are whispered about Inéz herself, and they are true, she says. She becomes an owl and circles above the countryside, where she can see everything, present, past, and future. Her monologue ends at dawn, when she tells Zapata she wants to look at him once again before he wakes and leaves her.

Commentary

Character Insight

The two major speakers in these stories (and there may be only two; the speaker in "Bread" may be Clemencia, who also narrates "Never Marry a Mexican"), although they exist in very dissimilar settings, are alike in several ways. Both see themselves as independent women, having to work to support themselves and rather happier than otherwise to be able to do so. Both see themselves as powerful, specifically within their relationships with the men in their lives, and the power of each consists of a kind of magic: Clemencia is a painter who can "make" and "remake" her art and her subjects; Inés is a witch who can see past and future as well as present. Yet both, at least in the monologues that make up the stories, seem to define themselves and their lives by their relationships to men. Each is bitter that she is not the central woman in the man's life, yet neither seems willing (or perhaps able) to end her relationship. Clemencia, especially, seems tied to her ex-lover to the point that she "circles around" him obsessively. Perhaps the reader finds this obsession less understandable in her case only because she has no children from the relationship, whereas Inés does have children with Zapata; Clemencia reveals that she has had affairs with other men, while Inés has not, but for each of these women her relationship with the man she addresses (Drew, Zapata) is obviously the central and only serious romantic relationship of her life.

Both women seem to define their relationships as *love*, and to both of them this seems to mean, among other things, holding power over their men. Each woman seems to compare and contrast her relationship with her lover to her relationship with her father. In each story, too, the narrator seems to emphasize a class difference between her and her lover—Clemencia is introduced to her lover's wife at an exhibition where the wife is a patron and the artist has brought her students; Inés remarks her father's dislike for Zapata who dresses in a flashy *"charro"* (cowboy) style in contrast to the peasant dress of the farmers. These contrasts are underlined in "Bread," where the non-Latino lover remarks upon the "charm" of a section of the city where the speaker's small cousin died from eating rat poison.

In each story, a central image is the gaze of the woman; she looks at the sleeping man and thus *possesses* him. In "Never Marry a Mexican," this is reinforced by the narrator's similar possession of her lover's son and by her use of one or both men as models in her painting, whereby others see them through her eyes.

In their structure, the two stories are very similar. Neither is a traditional linear narrative, and both deliberately blur the usual concept of time—past, present, and future. Inés, in her out-of-body travel, can see all times and places, and her "circling" over Zapata and their lives is, she says, literal. The artist also "circles," reliving past times, addressing Drew and his son alternately in a way that suggests they are sometimes, to her, the same person.

Glossary

[***Note:*** A number of the words in this section, used in "Eyes of Zapata," are from Nahuatl, a Native American language indigenous to central and western Mexico.]

fanfarrón   a braggart; a showoff.

carnitas   barbequed pork.

paletas   slices.

mundo sin fin, amen   world without end, amen.

Malinche (also *Malinalli, Malintzin, "Doña Marina"*)   historically, an Aztec woman, sold by her people as a slave to the Maya and later given as a gift to the *conquistador* Hernando Cortés; as Cortés' mistress, she played a huge role in the defeat of the Aztec empire by the Spanish, acting as interpreter and convincing the ruler Moteczoma (Montezuma II) to surrender. Malinche has been regarded as a traitor to her own people, although it is suggested that she acted out of revenge for their having sold her into slavery and also that by persuading the emperor to surrender she saved many lives; here (in "Never Marry a Mexican") Clemencia and her lover use her name playfully apparently in reference to their different skin colors, but the name has a cutting edge when one recalls that Malinalli's other name, Malinche, is used to mean a betrayer of her people.

mi doradita   my little brown girl.

mi trigueño, . . . chulito . . .   my dark one, . . . cute one . . . .

jaripeos   shows similar to rodeos, with demonstrations of horsemanship.

barrancas   deep gorges, precipices.

tan chistoso. Muy bonachón, muy bromista   so funny. Very good-natured, a real jokester.

"Tres vicios . . . y enamorado . . . ."   "Three vices I have, and they are deep-rooted in me: being a drunk, a gambler, and a lover." (Lyrics from *El Abandonado* ["The Abandoned One"], a popular song; see the Glossary for Part Four, later.)

petate   sleeping mat.

campesino   a small farmer; a peasant.

chachalaca   a pheasant (any bird flying into a house is an omen of death).

ayúdame   Help me.

"Ojos que no ven, corazón que no siente"   Literally, "Eyes that don't see, heart that doesn't feel"; i.e., better not to know.

milpas   cornfields.

jacales   small farm houses.

el porvenir   the future.

caciques   landowners; the political bosses or leaders.

metate   grinding stone.

huipil   a traditional hand-embroidered blouse.

guacamaya   macaw.

mujeriego   womanizer.

La madre tierra que nos mantiene y cuida   Mother earth who watches over us and supports us.

solteronas   unmarried women.

pulqueria   a *pulque* bar (*pulque* is a fermented drink made from cactus juice).

cielito de mi corazón   an affectionate phrase; literally, "little sky of my heart."

There Was a Man, There Was a Woman—Part Three

Anguiano Religious Articles . . . ; Little Miracles, Kept Promises; *Los* Boxers; There Was a Man, There Was a Woman

Summary

The speaker in the first of these stories (full title: "Anguiano Religious Articles Rosaries Statues Medals Incense Candles Talismans Perfumes Oils Herbs") goes into a religious articles store to get a picture or statue of the Virgin of Guadalupe, apparently to offer at a shrine for a very ill friend. The owner insults her when she can't decide what to buy. She says he's headed for hell.

"Little Miracles, Kept Promises" is a collection of 23 notes and letters, some accompanied by objects, left at a shrine (or perhaps several shrines) in a San Antonio church. These are both petitions and notes of thanksgiving, addressed to Christ, St. Mary, and various other saints, and dealing with a variety of human problems from a teenager's pimples to the painful illness of an old gentleman's wife. The final note is preceded by a short monologue in the voice of that note's writer, a young woman who has cut off her hair to signify that she rejects the traditional woman's role in life.

The elderly man who is the speaker in "*Los* Boxers" is doing his wash in a coin laundry, talking to a woman who is there with her very young daughter. He relates problems with his laundry and talks about his wife, who has died.

The section's title story tells (using third person and an omniscient narrator) of two lonely people, a man and woman, each of whom is paid every two weeks on Fridays. They go on payday to the same bar to drink with their friends, get relatively drunk, go home, and look sadly at the moon. Because they get paid on alternate Fridays, they have never met.

Commentary

This group of stories displays Cisneros' great talent for *voice*. The reader is introduced to several beautifully sketched characters in a few short pages: the tired middle-aged woman trying to decide how best to spend ten dollars—all the money she has—on a devotional article; the lonely widower talking to a stranger in a laundromat; even the writer of a one-line prayer who has fallen in love with a man not her husband and humbly begs God for help. Each of these stories, sketches, and letters invites us to consider the life of its central character or characters and to participate imaginatively in its fiction.

We must read carefully in order to do so; like much poetry, these pieces are precisely wrought. Although they seem casual, un-self-conscious, even artless (in the sense that they seem to *be* the unplanned discourse of their speakers), every word in each story counts, adding its deft stroke to the characterization. The exception is "There Was a Man, There Was a Woman," in which the parallel phrases and sentences very art*ful*ly delineate the loneliness of these two similar people. And loneliness is the thread that ties all of these stories together, along with human need and the dogged courage of the characters, who face their loneliness and hardships bravely, thankful for whatever they have and determined to make the best of what life has handed them.

Glossary

los amores de la calle   literally, "loves of the street"; streetwalkers, hookers.

Te ofrezco este . . . . Adela O.   "I offer you this photo of my children. Watch them, dear God, and if you take away the drinking of my son I promise I'll light candles. Help us with our bills, Lord, and that our income tax check may arrive soon so we can pay our bills. Give us a good life and please help our sons to change their ways. You who are so generous, listen to these requests that I ask of you with all my heart and all the faith of my soul. Have pity, my Lord. My name is Adela O.

Thank you *por el milagro* . . . . Thank you for the miracle of having me graduate from high school. Here I give you a picture of my graduation.

***Venimos desde* . . . .** We come from very far away. Infinite thanks, Lord. Thanks for having listened to us.

ven a saludar come and say hello.

quedar bien make a good impression.

"I wanted you bare-breasted, snakes in your hands . . . ." The speaker, Chayo, is here referring to a famous image of the Mother Goddess from the ancient bronze-age Minoan culture of Crete (c. 3000–c. 1100 B.C.).

There Was a Man, There Was a Woman—Part Four

Tin Tan Tan; *Bien* Pretty

Summary

The speaker of "Tin Tan Tan" is a young man, a poet (he will appear as a central character in "*Bien* Pretty") who is addressing his lost love in very flowery, melodramatic language. His poem, written in short paragraphs in the form of an acrostic (each paragraph begins with a letter of the woman's name), makes it quite clear that he is heartbroken and will probably die if she isn't moved to take him back.

The other side of this love affair is described in "*Bien* Pretty," whose narrator, Lupe, is the woman addressed in the preceding poem. Lupe, a painter, moved from San Francisco to San Antonio and is house-sitting for a fashionable artist; she hired an exterminator to get rid of the cockroaches and then hired him to pose for her, and they fell in love. In the midst of a passionate affair, he told her he had to return to Mexico to take care of something involving his children, and she eventually heard that he has two wives in two different Mexican cities. Now she really misses him but is trying to convince herself that she doesn't need him in order to be happy.

Commentary

Theme

"Tin Tan Tan" is a sort of overture to the book's final story, and together these two stories illustrate one of Cisneros' recurring themes, the two different worlds inhabited by a woman and a man—specifically, by a Chicana and the Mexican man with whom she can't help falling in love but with whom she cannot live and still retain her independent identity and self-respect.

Flavio's poem is utterly based on form, and what he says in it is so prescribed by tradition as to be clichéd; it purports to be a baring of his soul, but the reader recognizes that the poet either doesn't mean a word of it, really, or *is* actually suffering but cannot break out of his self-constructed "romantic" persona long enough to convey any real (as opposed to phony) emotion.

Lupe, his beloved, has come to San Antonio to help her recover from another, longer-term romance with a man who threw her over for a blonde. She is very much into traditional Latino culture and cannot help falling for Flavio's looks and masterful masculinity, but she is irritated when he points out that he really *is* Mexican and thus doesn't need to rely on various trappings, costumes, and so on. He would also like her to behave like a traditional Latino woman—that is, to be submissive, demure, ladylike—and she can't and/or won't comply. When he leaves, she is partly devastated, partly relieved.

Style & Language

Like "Never Marry a Mexican" and "Eyes of Zapata," "*Bien* Pretty" is told in a non-linear fashion by its narrator. Although the events of the main "story" (the love affair) are related more or less in chronological order, Lupe tells other things about herself and engages in related musings between and among these events; the effect of this narrative style is to suggest an unplanned, relatively shapeless, stream-of-consciousness exposition of both character and incident. Also as in those other two stories, the image of the woman's gaze (especially the *artist's* gaze) "possessing" the man—remaking him as her creature—appears here. Lupe, however, is less obsessed and much less bitter than Clemencia in "Never Marry a Mexican"; she seems, as the narrative ends, to be moving on with her life as an independent woman.

Glossary

"Me abandonaste, . . . el amor de Dios"   "You abandoned me, woman, because I'm very poor, / And for having the disgrace of being married. / What am I to do if I am the Abandoned One, / Abandoned I shall be, for the love of God." (From "*El Abandonado*" [by Jesus Martínez].)

"Ya me voy ,/ ay te dejo en San Antonio"   "Now I'm leaving, / O I leave you in San Antonio."

chaparritos   short people.

corajes   angers.

"La Cucuracha Apachurrada" "The Squashed Cockroach."

curandero medicine man; folk healer.

retablo alterpiece.

rebozos shawls.

Adiós y suerte Goodbye and good luck.

De poeta y loco todos tenemos un poco We all have a little of a poet and a crazy person in us.

Cuidate Take care.

Abrazos Hugs.

el baile de los viejitos the dance of the elders.

Regresa a Mi Return to Me; this is the name (and advertised effect) of a "magic" powder which Lupe has bought, she says, for the colorful design of its label.

lárgate get out.

Amar es Vivir To Love is to Live.

"Soy infeliz" I'm unhappy.

"Ya no. Es verdad que te adoro, pero más me adoro yo" "Not anymore. It's true I adore you, but I adore myself more."

tan tán the famous end to Mexican movies.

CHARACTER ANALYSES

Esperanza Cordero
(The House on Mango Street)

Esperanza is the most fully developed character in the book. All our information about her comes *from* her; some things she tells us directly (and we must be alert to the possibility that they are perhaps true only at the moment she says them), others indirectly in her reported actions, thoughts, and feelings. Some things about her we can never know, but because her voice is both direct and intimate, we can "know" her in some ways better than her friends and family do, better perhaps than she knows herself.

On one hand, Esperanza is a typical young adolescent girl, at some moments a child and at some an adult. She jumps rope with her friends, rides three on a bike, is drawn to a good Bugs Bunny cartoon. Very late in the book, she says of a neighbor, "I like Alicia because once she gave me a little leather purse with the word GUADALAJARA stitched on it . . ."—a very childish locution, for we know that Esperanza's feelings of liking and admiration for Alicia are not at all that simple.

On the other hand, this woman-child can exhibit very mature insights. Her assessments of Sally ("all you wanted was to love, . . . and no one could call that crazy") and of Marin ("waiting for a car to stop, a star to fall, someone to change her life"), for example, show her innate ability not only to recognize another person's motives but also to empathize with others, both signs of mental and emotional maturity. They are also signs of an imaginative intelligence that marks Esperanza as something more than average. She is a very bright girl who likes to read, to learn things and put new information together, to show off what she knows. Moreover, her intelligence is specifically creative, as is shown by her poetry, her originality, and especially her characteristic way of describing things in imaginative similes and other metaphors.

Perhaps it is Esperanza's imaginative intelligence that makes her suspect the traditional path to womanhood, through courtship and early marriage, of being a trap. It is a trap that draws her, of course; like most young girls, she feels herself becoming a sexual being, and she is impatient to get away from home, to stop being her parents' daughter and start being her own person. Doing this in the traditional way, she sees, would be dangerous. Finding a new way will be lonely and difficult, for she will have to swim against the current. But Esperanza is able to employ her natural adolescent impulses and feelings in this enterprise, channeling them into independence, ambition, and the courageous refusal to capitulate to social pressures towards conformity.

In order to make these transformations, Esperanza necessarily dramatizes herself somewhat, as when she decides to become "beautiful and cruel." Such self-dramatization really amounts to forming a mental image of herself that she can adjust as needed. Part of Esperanza's self-image is one of stoicism; she keeps her feelings to herself and actually— for the narrator of a book—*says* relatively little, leaving the reader to infer a great deal. In "Four Skinny Trees," she seems to be working on her self-image, rather enjoying her identification with the trees in what she sees as their strength, anger, and feeling of displacement. Only in "Red Clowns" does Esperanza actually break down—significantly, not to the reader but to her own mental picture of Sally—and characteristically she returns in the next chapter in her usual terse style, as if the incident had never happened. And, in the three short chapters at the end of the book, she reveals what we might already have guessed about her: Esperanza is a person who will feel everything very deeply and will quietly channel her experiences and feelings into creative energy; they will emerge transformed, as art.

Our knowledge of other characters also comes from Esperanza, who understands them on her own level; we can know more about them, in some cases, by combining what she says with our own insights into human nature. An example is one very minor character—Earl, the jukebox repairman who lives in a basement apartment near Esperanza. Esperanza knows some things about him and probably recognizes his loneliness and displacement, but as a child, she is still unable to articulate these things; older readers will see more than Esperanza does. Other minor characters (including some, like Lucy and Rachel, Nenny, even Esperanza's mother, who appear in more than one chapter) can be "analyzed" as well; the trick is to examine the character through Esperanza's eyes and at the same time to recognize—given our knowledge of who Esperanza is—the hints she gives us, almost unconsciously, of the character she does not yet see. (It is a measure of Cisneros' talent that these hints are almost always present, but that they never intrude upon the integrity of Esperanza's character.) Some of these characters, like Earl, are really minor; the others, important as they may be in Esperanza's life, are (typically for a girl her age) both taken for granted and dismissed from the front row of people with whom she is just now most concerned. The *really* important people to Esperanza are girls and young women whom she sees as possible role models, a little older than she, a little closer to womanhood.

Marin *(The House on Mango Street)*

Marin is a girl of about 13 or 14 whose parents have sent her to live with relatives in Chicago and whose relatives in Chicago would like to send her back to her parents. The adults' motive for wanting to be rid of Marin may very well be that she is trouble, a "boy-crazy" girl and potentially a bad influence on younger sisters and girl-cousins. Marin sneaks cigarettes, dresses seductively, and stares boldly back at boys. She goes out by herself to dances all over the city, probably sneaking out after her aunt has gone to bed and probably pretending to be older than she really is. She is an invaluable source of information on sex, cosmetics, and the ways of men, all those things Esperanza is curious about and cannot learn from books or from her mother. Esperanza's reports suggest that Marin herself, however, is not so well informed as she thinks she is; one suspects that her extreme youth and a sense of honor among the boys and men she dances with—along with a good deal of luck— have so far protected her.

For Marin's precocious sexual maturity is not promiscuity but simply the only way she knows—having learned from the movies and "romance" magazines that young girls of her time devoured—of looking for that magical key to everything: love. The mythic romantic story of true love like a bolt of lightning, sweet music, and wedding bells— popular in Western culture for centuries before Marin, and always ending with "happily ever after"—is what drives her, and she is young and innocent enough to believe it. Even Marin cannot explain why she waited at the hospital for a young man whose last name she doesn't know, but the answer is simple: She stayed with Geraldo out of the pure love in her romantic heart.

Sally *(The House on Mango Street)*

Sally, perhaps even younger than Marin, is not so innocent, for— although "romance" (that is, falling in love and getting married) is part of the sexual game she plays—she has a more urgent reason to play it. Like Marin, she wishes to be taken away by a man; unlike the other girl, Sally needs to be rescued from a home life that has turned into a nightmare. Sally's aunts ran away from home with men, thus bringing "shame" upon their family. The fact that they were probably driven to leave in the same way that Sally is driven makes no difference; it is, according to the tradition in which Sally's father is steeped, a woman's responsibility to remain pure until her wedding day. This means that she must not behave provocatively, and because (as he knows, being a man) almost any female behavior is provocative, she must be warned and punished frequently.

Sally's father beats her with his fists, his belt. In his defense, it should be said that he probably does love Sally; he himself is driven by sexual and cultural forces he has no way of understanding, and, not understanding them, he perpetuates them into another generation. Sally's mother abets him, lies for him, treats Sally's cuts and bruises, and allows the cycle to continue. Sally sees only one way out: She must find a man who will marry her. In order to do this, she fights with her long-time "best friend" (significantly it is a physical fight; physical violence is what Sally knows) and betrays Esperanza's friendship. And when Sally finds a husband, he turns out to be as violent, as jealous, as controlling, and as ignorant as her father—but then, what else might be expected of someone who would marry a desperate 13-year-old?

Alicia *(The House on Mango Street)*

The character who has the most positive influence upon Esperanza is her neighbor Alicia, a college student who—by the end of the book— seems to have become Esperanza's good friend. Perhaps surprisingly, Alicia is less well developed as a character than Sally or even Marin. All we know of her is that she has lived in the neighborhood for a while, that she is the daughter of a traditional widowed Latino father (meaning she is expected to do all the housework), that she lives in a run-down apartment (meaning her father goes to work, comes home, and does little else), and that despite being terribly busy and tired, Alicia makes time to talk with a 12- or 13-year-old neighbor girl, Esperanza.

From this small store of information, then, we can deduce something of Alicia's character: She is strong, determined, ambitious. She knows what Esperanza spends the period of this book finding out: that the traditional role for a woman—little education, early marriage and children—is all too often a trap lined with unhappiness. And she is kindhearted and wise enough to recognize a kindred spirit in Esperanza. Perhaps the reason Esperanza says so little about Alicia is that she too recognizes this likeness and extends her own somewhat secretive minimalism to this sensitive, tough-hearted young woman, an older version of herself.

"Ixchel" ("One Holy Night")

Most of the narrators of the *"Woman Hollering Creek"* stories are named in the stories; the exceptions are one who seems to be a middle-aged woman, in "Anguiano Religious Articles," an elderly man in *"Los Boxers,"* the child-narrators of "My Lucy Friend Who Smells Like Corn," "Mexican Movies," and "Barbie-Q"—and "Ixchel," the narrator of "One Holy Night," who is in some ways herself a child, in others an ageless woman, representative of some mystical and mythical female principle. The only name by which she identifies herself in the story is that given her by her beloved, Boy Baby, who says his own true name is "Chaq Uxmal Paloquín" and that he is chosen to be the father of a boy who will restore the ancient glory of the Maya people.

Of course, as "Ixchel" and her grandmother learn from Boy Baby's sister, a Carmelite nun, her lover is a man almost 40 years old with no Mayan blood, an accused murderer of women. Seen from her grandmother's point of view, "Ixchel" is a very young girl who has been taken advantage of by a bad man; the grandmother blames not her but her lover—and her uncle Lalo, who ought to have been working on Saturdays himself so that his niece would not have been exposed to the evils that can overcome a girl on the city streets. "Ixchel's" own mother was similarly taken advantage of and was sent to the United States to have her baby, who seems to have been raised from birth by this grandmother. She has been brought up in a very traditional, old-fashioned (but seemingly not terribly strict)—and loving—Mexican style, against which she seems not to have rebelled at all, despite the fact that she is a young teenager living in Chicago. At 13 or 14, her voice is that of a rather sweet, simple-hearted (but not simple-minded) child. When her grandmother takes her out of school, she is happy to be staying home, learning to do fancy crocheting.

In another way, however, "Ixchel" is a woman grown. She knows the secret of sex, which to her is both "no big deal" and the great difference of her life. She identifies with all women and speaks to her curious little cousins in Mexico as if they were inhabitants of another world, light-years away from hers. She has been different from other girls all along, which is why she did not want to lose her virginity in an alley or some car; now she is, ironically, both different from other women and the same as all women, for she has accepted the mythical truth given her by her lover—and she knows that "life will always be hard."

"Ixchel's" very traditional upbringing may have contributed to her childlike simplicity, but her simplicity in turn is probably what has allowed her to be content with that upbringing. She has no difficulty accepting what Boy Baby says as the truth—even after she has learned that in an ordinary sense it is not true at all. This acceptance of two "truths" at once seems to be related to her acceptance of her lover's unconventional approach to time, according to which past and future and present are all in some way the same thing. She *accepts* these things without *understanding* them, nor does she feel any need to understand them on an intellectual level. This may be what protected her from Boy Baby, for if he is rightly accused of multiple killings, he certainly had every opportunity to kill "Ixchel" when she went with him to his apartment, when he wept and showed her an entire arsenal of guns and knives. Perhaps he recognized her as an inhabitant of a mythical world. And, indeed, the world she inhabits is one that rejects logic. Her world is one of *love*, which she sees not as romance nor as sexual pleasure but instead as a kind of atmosphere within which she exists, breathing it in and out like the man (significantly, a "crazy") who went around always with a harmonica in his mouth, making a kind of monotonous music with his breath.

Cleófilas ("Woman Hollering Creek")

The book's title story is told not by a character but by a third-person narrator who has access to its central character's thoughts and feelings and presents them in that character's inner language. Thus readers can observe Cleófilas through what other characters say about her (the women going to her wedding and Graciela), but also—and mainly—through her own thoughts and observations. What we learn is that she is a conventional young woman who possesses a certain depth of character that she herself discovers only when she is tested.

To begin with, Cleófilas seems rather shallow and unobservant. She knows how characters on soap operas dress and behave, but she agrees to marry a man she scarcely knows; Juan Pedro is a nonentity, but he lives and works across the border in Texas, he has a nice truck, and he has selected *her* as his bride, all of which makes him acceptable as a husband. She sees it all through a haze of *telenovelas* and romance novels; the creek, as she first crosses it, is "full of happily ever after." Only after she has married does she actually look at the man and begin to muse upon the fact that she has promised to spend her life with him.

At first she is simply stunned, not only by his physical violence but also by his manners, his selfishness and crassness, and his friends. He hurts, offends, and bores her. She is married to him, however, so she accepts her life like the conventional, well-brought-up girl she is. But as time goes by, rather than becoming inured to her situation, she becomes more observant, and what she observes is violence against women as a way of life—casual, accepted, part of the language. It is as if the part of her mind that was filled with fluff is now free to take in reality. At the same time, she must try to survive her situation: dependent, friendless, responsible for her child, and in mortal danger. This effort brings her perilously close to "the darkness under the trees"; suicide and infanticide are never named in the story but are always there in her ideas of La Llorona, the Weeping Woman who drowns her children.

The apparent turning point for Cleófilas is an "accident"—she reveals her problem to a nurse, who enlists a friend to help. But we know that there has been preparation for this, for Cleófilas doesn't begin to lie to the nurse (as she has told her husband she would) and has managed to save enough money to buy her own bus ticket home. The *conscious* turning point comes in Felice's pickup truck. Until this moment, Cleófilas has assumed that because she is a woman she must be passive, *re*act rather than act (as "La Gritona" must either be angry or in pain); now the realization that she can be in charge of her own life enters her, and it comes in the form of a laugh that feels to her like a freeing of water.

Rosario (Chayo) De Leon ("Little Miracles, Kept Promises")

Chayo appears as the speaker of a monologue/prayer before the last note of the story. In a sense she may also figure in other Cisneros fiction—not as the same character, specifically, but as a character only slightly different from Clemencia in "Never Marry a Mexican," Lupe in "*Bien* Pretty," Micaela of "'Mericans" (and probably of "Tepeyac"), even Alicia and Esperanza of *The House on Mango Street*. She is a university student, specifically an art student, who is defying culture and family by going to school and who (in Chayo's case) has angered and hurt her mother and grandmother by rejecting the traditional woman's role of wife and mother.

Just as seriously, Chayo has rejected Catholicism (with its attendant devotion to the Virgin Mary, especially strong in the Latin Church), causing her family to believe she is a hell-bound heretic. It is this facet of her defiance of tradition that is the subject of her prayer. By learning something of her people's past (Mexican history, the organization and strike of farm laborers in the U.S.), she has seen that devotion to the Virgin, which she had always associated with passivity and sorrow (her grandmother's sad prayers), might have a real potential for power. By learning something of ancient religions—including those of Mexico—she has begun to realize that the Mother Goddesses and the Virgin of Guadalupe are perhaps really the same figure. She has, she says, learned all of the Virgin's names, learned to see her in all her facets. Now, instead of a lonely defiance, Chayo has the power of her devotion (which is that of her family's tradition but much more besides) to back her up, and it has given her strength. As a symbol of this newfound strength, she has cut off her long braid of hair and offered it to the Virgin in thanks.

CRITICAL ESSAYS

Themes in Cisneros' Fiction

One way of reading Sandra Cisneros' fiction is to examine some of the central themes it seems repeatedly to deal with, several of which inform both *The House on Mango Street* and *"Woman Hollering Creek" and Other Stories*. Three of the most striking are sexual love as an exercise of power; alienation and displacement; and conflicts between the individual and cultural/familial tradition. These themes seem to be interrelated in that the first and second named grow directly out of the third.

Love as Power

The theme of love as power is most apparent in some of the *"Woman Hollering Creek"* stories, but it appears even in *Mango Street*, in the lives of Esperanza's acquaintances and in her own youthful experience. Rafaela, Minerva, *Mamacita*, and Sally—after her marriage—are all overpowered by their husbands, physically or otherwise, as a matter of course. Whatever the relationship between her own parents, it seems that Esperanza sees a normal love-and-marriage relationship as one in which the man holds and exercises complete power over "his" woman. The only alternative, she believes, would have the woman holding complete power. In "Beautiful and Cruel" she decides that she prefers that option, but a possible relationship in which power is held equally by both partners, a more-or-less equal give-and-take relationship, or even one in which power is *not* a major factor (or weapon) seems not to occur to her. Interestingly, the love-equals-power relationship is figured here in several instances as visual *gaze*: Boys stare at Marin, and she boldly returns the gaze; Sire looks at Esperanza, and she affects not to be frightened; women who have been disempowered (or who have never had any power) look out through a window at what they cannot have.

In the *"Woman Hollering Creek"* stories the love-equals-power theme is further explored, with Juan Pedro in the title story seeing Cleófilas, taking her from her father, and beginning to hold complete power over her. Other women protagonists, however (and one man, Tristán in "Remember the Alamo"), exercise the "beautiful and cruel" option, keeping power in their own hands and in their *gaze*—even, in the cases of Clemencia in "Never Marry a Mexican" and Lupe in *"Bien* Pretty,"* extending that power by "possessing" their men in their art and in effect distributing it to others who look at the men's images in their paintings.

Alienation and Displacement

Another important theme in both books is the individual's feeling of alienation or displacement. Esperanza in *Mango Street* expresses the feeling often, saying she does not "belong" where she is and that she wishes she were from somewhere else—although Alicia assures her that she "is Mango Street" and will carry it with her when she leaves there. In the *"Woman Hollering Creek"* stories, various characters' express similar feelings: the speakers in "'Mericans" and "Tepeyac"; Cleófilas in the title story, who first longs to get away from her hometown to Seguin, Texas, and then longs to be away from Seguin; and all the characters who feel alienated from each other and even from themselves. These last named include Clemencia, Lupe, and especially Tristán, who is so self-alienated he has created a new identity for himself, refers to himself (by his new name) in third person, and wishes to separate himself completely from the person he was in the past.

Individualism versus Cultural Traditions

Both of these themes—that of love-as-power and that of alienation—seem to proceed from the third and larger theme of the individual's conflict with a tradition that is both cultural and familial. Almost every female character in both books experiences the intensely potent force of this tradition influencing her to follow her Latino family tradition into marriage, when she would cease to "belong" to her father and begin to "belong" to her husband. Most of those who do not resist this force are portrayed as unhappy in the world they inhabit, from Esperanza's mother, who is "self-alienated" to the extent that she has not been able to utilize her artistic gifts and interests, to young women like Sally, Minerva, and Cleófilas, who are trapped in marriages to brutal men.

Those who *do* resist it are likely to remain partly (and unhappily) within the tradition, in that their relationships with the opposite sex are still power struggles. To the extent that they are successful in their resistance, they remain unhappily alienated from their own cultural roots and the feelings of loyalty they cannot eradicate. One such woman is Inés in "Eyes of Zapata," who left her father for Zapata and later gained a kind of independence from *him* (at least in a material sense, mostly because he ignored her for long periods), but who is still tied to her lover in their love-as-a-power-struggle relationship. Another is

Clemencia, who heeded her mother's advice *not* to follow tradition, but who then became alienated from her mother and involved in a long, obsessive "love" affair with a married man (who, ironically, is attracted to her cultural identity as a "Mexican" but would never divorce his wife and marry her *because* of that identity). Tristán, of course, is separated from his cultural tradition by his homosexuality; he clings to what he can of it in his art, as a performer of traditional dances, and he both mocks and pays tribute to tradition by utilizing a kind of male "drag"— an exaggeration of the masterful, powerful, intensely masculine Latino persona.

The only characters who seem to be able to avoid the double-bind of love-as-power and/or alienation are those who find a strength *within* their tradition that allows them to exist as self-respecting individuals. One such is "Ixchel" in "One Holy Night," who has become (in her own mind) sort of an embodiment of the ancient mythos into which her lover—himself *deeply* alienated, to the point of probable insanity— initiated her. Raised in a very traditional household and apparently happy there, she easily made the transition into an older tradition— and is saved, by her lover's physical and effectively complete disappearance from her life, from having to reconcile the myth with mundane existence. "Ixchel" achieved independence, power, and a sense of centeredness, of being where she belongs, by in effect going *into* tradition and coming out the other side. Another apparently fortunate character is Chayo of "Little Miracles, Kept Promises," who has discovered a link between her familial/cultural tradition and a broader world-mythos that allows her to participate in the power of the virgin/mother goddesses (including, as she sees it, the Virgin of Guadalupe/Mother of Christ) and to be both independent and centered in her own place.

Form and Language as Characterization in Cisneros' Fiction

Critics praise Sandra Cisneros' fiction for, among other things, her use of non-linear form and her colorful, image-rich language. Both are seen as evidence of her departure from traditional (patriarchal, white European-American) conventions of fiction in English in favor of a feminist, specifically Latina mode of discourse. I would argue that Cisneros uses both, as well, to accomplish her many-layered and exceptionally economical characterizations.

Cisneros' characters "come to life" often in remarkably few words, allowing the reader to feel both a sympathy with and a sense of individuality in almost every character that give even short sketches unusual depth and clarity. One way she achieves this dimensionality is by having her characters (often first-person narrators) think or speak (or, occasionally, write) in a way that reveals the shapes of their thought processes. The result is a sort of stream-of-consciousness discourse that can range from barely-conscious, extremely private "thoughts" or feelings through relatively public statements, as in the notes to the Virgin in "Little Miracles, Kept Promises." And one of the characteristics of such discourse is that even when it sets out to tell a linear narrative, other thoughts and feelings intervene to reshape the straight line into loops and disjunctive digressions. Because this is how most people seem to think unless they are deliberately using linear logic, we are invited to find the character's thought processes familiar and to identify with them.

Further, the shape of a character's thought processes helps to define her or him as an individual. Inés, in "Eyes of Zapata," sees herself as a witch in the form of an owl, circling all night around her life, outside any linear perception of time; Clemencia, in "Never Marry a Mexican," seems to be almost literally living in the past as well as the present as she too "circles" in time, addressing sometimes her ex-lover and sometimes his son; the speaker in "*Los* Boxers" tells us less about his loneliness in what he says than in the indirect way he says it. The rejection of linear form in favor of a more relaxed discourse is especially important in characterizing Esperanza of *The House on Mango Street*, for it creates an ironic tension between the narrator's idiosyncratic ordering and emphases and the reader's reception of her narrative, which in turn allows the reader to learn who the character is "as a person" in much the same way we learn to "know" actual people with whose thought processes we become familiar.

If the shape and direction of discourse is one way of discovering character, another is diction, including the images and figures of speech that distinguish a person's language. It is clear that Sandra Cisneros has a gift for colorful, imaginative language, but if we look closely at her fiction, we find that she uses different kinds of image and figure (or sometimes their absence) to portray different characters. The speaker of "One Holy Night," for example, uses similes and other figures sparely, and not at all in connection with everyday matters, but those she does use are rich in images that are both arcane and mystic, suggestive of the ancient mythos into which she says Boy Baby initiated her: She wanted her virginity to "come undone like gold thread, like a tent full of birds"; her lover's words are "like broken clay, . . . hollow sticks, . . . the swish of old feathers crumbling into dust." In contrast, the tough-talking speaker of "My *Tocaya*" uses two figurative expressions in her story: the thought that Max Lucas Luna might suddenly appear "makes [her] blood laugh," and the "ass" of said young man is "wrapped up neat and sweet like a Hershey bar." Nothing could make plainer the difference between these two girls, the first simple but otherworldly, the second conventional and mundane.

Speakers like the middle-aged woman in "Anguiano Religious Articles" and the elderly man in "*Los* Boxers" use no real figures of speech at all, as if their tiredness, or perhaps their long practice of conventionality, had depleted them of the gift of metaphor. On the other hand, "Rogelio Velasco" (a.k.a. Flavio Munguía) in "Tin Tan Tan" uses one tired, trite, and generally badly mixed metaphor after another, so awkwardly that they are unintentionally funny ("now that you have yanked my golden dreams from me, I shiver from this chalice of pain like a tender white flower tossed in rain"); when he ventures to coin his own figure, this poet with a tin ear unfortunately decides to allude to the circumstances under which he and his Lupe met: "Perhaps I can exterminate the pests of doubt . . . ."

Finally, Cisneros characters who are *really* imaginative artists use a language that is original, unique to each as an individual, and pleasingly concrete. For example, Chayo, of "Little Miracles, Kept Promises," uses metaphor to color a catalog of specific images: "Silk roses, plastic roses . . . Caramel-skinned woman in a white graduation cap and gown . . . Teenager with a little bit of herself sitting on her lap . . . ." She says her cut-off braid is "the color of coffee in a glass" and compares it to "the donkey tail in a birthday game"; her figures are complex, concrete, and unforced. Clemencia, in "Never Marry a Mexican," uses perhaps fewer figures (and fewer original ones) than the other artist-characters, and this may be because she is bitter and unhappy; her emotions may deplete her creative imagination. Still when she does speak figuratively, her language can be intensely original, as when she describes her relationship to her mother after her father's death by comparing it wrenchingly to a pet bird's injured leg, which eventually dried up and fell off. The bird "was fine, really," she concludes, her brisk assessment in painful contrast to her description of the injury. And, in contrast to Clemencia, Lupe of

"*Bien* Pretty" uses a wide range of figurative imagery, from her mock-horrific description of the cockroaches' "cannibal rites" to her metaphors for the Spanish language ("That sweep of palm leaves and fringed shawls. That startled fluttering, like the heart of a goldfinch . . .") that recall "Ixchel's" myth-like utterances.

Like Chayo's figures, but more playful and less grown-up, are those we find on practically every page of *The House on Mango Street*. Esperanza talks of cats "asleep like donuts," a big, clumsy dog "like a man dressed in a dog suit," hips on a maturing girl "ready and waiting like a new Buick with the keys in the ignition," two little black dogs "that leap and somersault like an apostrophe and comma." Her figures are more frequent and colorful when she is happy, fewer and farther between when she is not. And, appropriately, Esperanza's figures of speech, even when they are so wildly far-fetched as to be almost conceits (a Cadillac's smashed "nose" is "pleated like an alligator's"), are almost always similes, the simplest, least "mature," form of metaphor.

Thus form, in Cisneros' fiction, seems to exist primarily not for its own sake, nor to further any theoretical or political program, but for the very respectable purpose of advancing the sketches and portraits of that fiction's characters. Both in the non-linear shapes of the pieces and in the language of the characters themselves, form is here a means to the end of making these human sketches and portraits come to life.

CliffsNotes Review

Use this CliffsNotes Review to test your understanding of the original text and reinforce what you've learned in this book. After you work through the review and essay questions, identify the quote section, and the fun and useful practice projects, you're well on your way to understanding a comprehensive and meaningful interpretation of *The House on Mango Street* and *"Woman Hollering Creek" and Other Stories*.

Q&A

1. Near the beginning of *The House on Mango Street*, Esperanza's neighbor Cathy says her family is moving because:

   a. The neighborhood is "getting bad."

   b. They have inherited a lot of money.

   c. Cats are no longer allowed in their building.

   d. Her parents are getting a divorce.

2. Esperanza's mother quit school before she graduated, she tells Esperanza, because:

   a. She had a fight with her best friend.

   b. She wanted to get married.

   c. She'd failed her history exam.

   d. She was ashamed of her clothes.

3. The narrator of the story "My *Tocaya*" calls Patricia Benavídez her *tocaya* because the other girl:

   a. Is her second cousin.

   b. Has the same first name as the narrator.

   c. Has agreed to fix the narrator up with her brother.

   d. Is her sworn enemy.

4. Cleófilas, in the story "Woman Hollering Creek," married the Texan Juan Pedro Martínez Sánchez because:

   a. She was pregnant and her father insisted.

   b. She was tired of living with her father and brothers, and she wanted a romantic adventure.

c. Her best friend was in love with him and Cleófilas wanted to make her jealous.

d. He had threatened to kill her unless she married him.

5. In the story *"Bien* Pretty," Lupe's only problem with the house she's staying in is that:

a. The kitchen roof leaks.

b. It isn't furnished.

c. The furnace is broken.

d. It's infested with cockroaches.

Answers: (1) a. (2) d. (3) b. (4) b. (5) d.

Identify the Quote

Identify the speaker, the work (*The House on Mango Street* or one of the *"Woman Hollering Creek"* stories), and if possible the situation (what is the speaker talking about, or whom is she/he addressing?):

1. Everyone is capable of becoming a traitor, and traitors must be broken, you say. A horse to be broken. A new saddle that needs breaking in. To break a spirit. Something to whip and lasso like you did in the *jaripeos* years ago.

2. Then the visitors came . . . in and out of the little house. Anyone who had ever wondered what color the walls were came and came to look at that little thumb of a human in a box like candy.

3. I'm going to have five children. Five. Two girls. Two boys. And one baby. [. . .] My baby will be named Alegre, because life will always be hard.

Answers: (1) [In "Eyes of Zapata," Inés is addressing the sleeping Emiliano, telling him the kind of man he has become—or perhaps has always been.] (2) [In *The House on Mango Street*, Esperanza describes the reception and viewing in Lucy and Rachel's house for their baby sister who has died.] (3) [In "One Holy Night," the narrator, waiting for her baby to be born, is thinking about her future.]

Essay Questions

1. Write a reflective essay on your own name (first, middle, last, or all of them). Where did it come from? What does it mean? What does it mean *to you*? Do you like it or dislike it (or both)? Why? Some people have never thought much about their own names; if you have not, do some thinking and some research, if necessary, before writing. But make your first draft as wide-ranging and spontaneous as you can, to let your real feelings about your name come through.

2. Describe as clearly as you can one of the first good times you can remember having with a friend or friends in your childhood. Think about it first, and then try to make the descriptive narrative as immediate and concrete as possible, the way Esperanza narrates her experience with Lucy and Rachel in "Our Good Day."

3. Write an essay analyzing one of the characters (or narrators) from a story in *"Woman Hollering Creek" and Other Stories*. What is important to the character and what is not? What motivates him or her to act? What does she or he like, dislike, and why? What do *you* like or admire, and what do you dislike, about the character? Base your analysis on whatever evidence you can find in the story *and* on your own best guesses. You may choose a fairly well developed character, or if you want to you can choose a very minor character and, still using whatever evidence you can find, write an imaginative analysis.

Practice Projects

1. Do some research in Mexican folklore or mythology and find a short story or tale that might be adapted for young children, one with two or more characters. Develop a dramatic skit from this story, write a script, cast the parts, make costumes and any necessary props, and present your skit to an audience. (This could be a class or group project.)

2. Follow the suggestion above, using a story from the folklore or mythology of some other region or ethnic group.

3. Draw (or paint, sculpt, etc.) a picture or other visual illustration, either representational or abstract, based on a character or incident from *The House on Mango Street* or *"Woman Hollering Creek" and Other Stories*. (This, too, could be a class or group project; the results might be presented at an exhibit using the next suggestion.)

4. Find some of the recordings of Latin music mentioned in "*Bien* Pretty" (or other Latin music) and make a tape or CD in which these are interspersed with short readings from Cisneros' books recorded by class members.

CliffsNotes Resource Center

The learning doesn't need to stop here. CliffsNotes Resource Center shows you the best of the best—links to the best information in print and online about the author and/or related works. And don't think that this is all we've prepared for you; we've put all kinds of pertinent information at www.cliffsnotes.com. Look for all the terrific resources at your favorite bookstore or local library and on the Internet. When you're online, make your first stop www.cliffsnotes.com where you'll find more incredibly useful information about *The House on Mango Street* and *"Woman Hollering Creek" and Other Stories*.

Books

This CliffsNotes book provides a meaningful interpretation of *The House on Mango Street* and *"Woman Hollering Creek" and Other Stories*. If you are looking for information about the author and/or related works, check out these other publications:

Prehistoric Mesoamerica, by Richard E. W. Adams. A thorough anthropological study of pre-Columbian peoples in the region that encompasses modern Mexico, Guatemala, Honduras, El Salvador, and Belize. Newer studies are available, but Adams' book is invaluable for its straightforward, readable style. Includes bibliography, glossaries, maps, and many illustrations. Boston: Little, Brown, 1977.

Latina Self-Portraits: Interviews with Contemporary Women Writers, edited by Bridget Kevane and Juanita Heredia. Lively interviews with Latina writers, including an interesting and informative one with Cisneros that sheds light on *Mango Street* and the *"Woman Hollering Creek"* stories as well as on Cisneros' poems, her family, and the writer herself. Albuquerque: University of New Mexico Press, 2000.

Quetzalcóatl and Guadalupe: The Formation of Mexican National Consciousness 1531-1813, by Jacques Lafaye. Forward by Octavio Paz; translated from the French by Benjamin Keen. An imaginative historical study concerned with how myth and history inform Mexico's national development. This book may be too deep for many students; however, it addresses interestingly the connection between Tonantzín and the Virgin of Guadalupe made by Cisneros in "Little Miracles, Kept Promises." Chicago: University of Chicago Press, 1976 (first published as Quetzalcóatl et Guadalupe, 1974).

Everything You Need to Know about Latino History, by Himilce Novas. Fascinating—and aptly titled—source, with question-and-answer format, by a Cuban-born writer who asks (and answers) questions about Latino history and culture, in and out of the U.S. New York: Plume, 1994.

Americanos: Latino Life in the United States, by Edward James Olmos, Lea Ybarra, and Manuel Monterrey. Introduction by Carlos Fuentes. A book full of wonderful photos, color and black-and-white, depicting Latinos in the U.S. It has a bilingual preface and introduction. Boston: Little, Brown, 1999.

It's easy to find books published by IDG Books Worldwide, Inc. You'll find them in your favorite bookstores (on the Internet and at a store near you). We also have three Web sites that you can use to read about all the books we publish:

- www.cliffsnotes.com
- www.dummies.com
- www.idgbooks.com

Internet

Check out these Web resources for more information about Sandra Cisneros and *The House on Mango Street* and *"Woman Hollering Creek" and Other Stories*:

Encarta Online: Cisneros, Sandra, http://encarta.msn.com/find/Concise.asp?ti=0AB74000—This page provides a brief biography of the author. Related links and periodical articles are available with Encarta membership.

Cisneros, Sandra: Interview, http://acunix.wheatonma.edu/rpearce/MultiC_Web/Authors/Sandra_Cisneros/body_sandra_cisneros.html—Wheaton College conducted an interview with Cisneros in which she talks about the influence and use of Spanish language in her writing.

Cisneros, Sandra—lasmujeres.com, www.lasmujeres.com/cisneros.htm—This page features a *Publisher's Weekly* article and a biography. Find additional information about other Chicana authors through the provided links.

Cisneros, Sandra: Teacher Resource File, http://nsd.k12.mi.us/~amlit/third/Sandra.htm—This site offers a collection of resources for someone teaching Cisneros' books and includes bibliography, lesson plans, and more.

Next time you're on the Internet, don't forget to drop by www.cliffsnotes.com. We created an online Resource Center that you can use today, tomorrow, and beyond.

Magazines and Journals

Carbonell, Ana Maria. "From Llorona to Gritona: Coatlicue in Feminist Tales by Viramontes and Cisneros." Melus. Summer 1999, vol. 24, iss. 2, pp. 53–73. Carbonell discusses the figure of La Llorona in Mexican folklore, her connection with the goddess Coatlicue, and the function of this figure in two stories by Chicanas (the second of which is "Woman Hollering Creek").

Sanchez, Reuben. "Remembering Always to Come Back: The Child's Wished-for Escape and the Adult's Empowered Return in Sandra Cisneros' House on Mango Street." Children's Literature. Annual 1995, vol. 23, pp. 221–42. Interesting discussion of Mango Street and the character of Esperanza.

Send Us Your Favorite Tips

In your quest for knowledge, have you ever experienced that sublime moment when you figure out a trick that saves time or trouble? Perhaps you realized you were taking ten steps to accomplish something that could have taken two. Or you found a little-known workaround that achieved great results. If you've discovered a useful resource that gave you insight into or helped you understand *The House on Mango Street* and *"Woman Hollering Creek" and Other Stories* and you'd like to share it, the CliffsNotes staff would love to hear from you. Go to our Web site at www.cliffsnotes.com and click the Talk to Us button. If we select your tip, we may publish it as part of Cliffs Notes Daily, our exciting, free e-mail newsletter. To find out more or to subscribe to a newsletter, go to www.cliffsnotes.com on the Web.

Index